WINNING WITH IP

MANAGING INTELLECTUAL PROPERTY TODAY

OPENING UP NEW PATHS TO GROWTH

Winning with IP: Managing intellectual property today

Third edition published for Newsdesk Global Communications by Novaro Publishing Ltd, Techno Centre, Coventry University Technology Park, Puma Way, Coventry CV1 2TT e: publish@novaropublishing.com.

© Newsdesk Global Communications,
Novaro Publishing and individual contributors, 2022, 2021, 2019

ISBN: 978-1-7398640-2-6
E-ISBN: 978-1-7398640-3-3

A CIP catalogue record for this book is available from the British Library.

Designed by Chantel Barnett, Clear Design CC Ltd

For further details about our authors and our titles, see:
www.novaropublishing.com

WINNING WITH IP

MANAGING INTELLECTUAL PROPERTY TODAY

OPENING UP NEW PATHS TO GROWTH

CONSULTANT EDITOR

ADAM JOLLY

Newsdesk Global
Independent Book Publishers

NOVARO
PUBLISHING

CONSULTANT EDITOR

Adam Jolly is a business writer, editor and publisher who specializes in growth, innovation, technology and leadership. He has produced titles for many leading organizations and has written extensively about the challenges facing entrepreneurs, innovators and directors. Recent titles have been described as 'at the cutting edge of real-time digital innovation' by EasyJet and as 'an ideal manual for ambitious entrepreneurs' by StartUp Britain.

CONTENTS

FOREWORD

What characterises managing intellectual property today? From deep tech to inventing with artificial intelligence and its correlation to personalized medicine to the internet of things, connectivity and standard essential patents, the range of technology driving innovation growth is vast. Yet considerations need to be focused and nuanced for high-growth companies seeking their niche as they evolve. The forms of IP for ownership and protection too may change as the traditional categories shift, as we are seeing in the metaverse and digital wallets. These IP landscapes all have an impact on the value being built and how the competing demands for human and financial resources are resolved as companies grow rapidly.

The various themes covered in this book reflect the different facets that high-growth technology businesses (HTBs) need to understand, assimilate and adopt as appropriate. Practical and concrete examples for commercialization and deployment of IP are found in the chapters on four tech licensing business models and on collaborations. The view on IP risk for investors is pertinent and so is freedom to grow. Knowing whether you are building to grow versus building to sell makes a difference to how a business achieves a successful and profitable exit. Each theme is well explored and much needed within the context of how HTBs have to keep up or be left behind in this fast-paced competitive world, accelerated by the pandemic, disrupted supply chains, escalating energy costs and the increasing focus on environment, sustainability and governance (ESG) obligations.

Challenges for HTBs are ever evolving. Too many fail, because the landscape changed without them noticing. I greatly welcome this excellent book, as it is one I can foresee HTBs picking up firstly to get a sense of trends, then again and again to dive deep into issues of specific concern or interest for rich learnings, direction and clarity in steps to improve the odds of success with proprietary technology, brands and better IP management – in short, winning with IP.

Audrey Yap
Managing director, Yusarn Audrey LLC
Past president, LESI and co-chair, HTB committee
Chair, Singapore Innovation and Productivity Institute

1.
IP STANDARDS FOR
A DIGITAL AGE

Digital transformation makes new demands on IP management.
Two recent standards are seeking to bring everyone up to speed.
A CEIPI report reviews progress

No industrial company and hardly any high-growth technology business can ignore the terms Industry 4.0, the Fourth Industrial Revolution or the internet of things (IoT) anymore. Just as software-based solutions are constantly being updated and improved, businesses have been reinventing themselves again and again for hundreds of years. We can already look back on three industrial revolutions. Industry 4.0 joins the ranks, forcing companies to adapt to a fast-changing business environment[1].

Those who want to gain competitive advantages are developing new business models, use cases and applications with significant digital components. Intelligent platforms are changing the way we interact with customers. In production, the use of new communication standards (eg, 5G), cloud computing, artificial intelligence and digital twins is closing the gap between software and hardware, leading to greater agility and higher efficiency in the industrial internet of things (IIoT)[2].

Digitalization and the resulting changes in business ecosystems[3] are leading to a radical rethink of the way intellectual property is handled, especially patents. Companies have always tried not only to secure their own range of services legally by patenting their technical developments, but also to gain exclusive market positions by designing patent portfolios that are specifically geared towards customer benefits. Such IP strategies allow for the expansion of your own market share and many other advantages. New business partners, markets and competitors, including those from other industries, bring opportunities and risks whose complexity even larger companies cannot master comprehensively.

Typical digital interaction patterns for creating customer benefits, such as condition monitoring, pre-emptive maintenance or updating mobile devices over the air from the cloud, are covered by a large number of patents that are increasing rapidly worldwide. For those making innovations in physical products or in transaction-based business models, adaptations to how they organize the development of their patents may be smaller.

To sum up, the new developments in the technological and economic area, related to Industry 4.0 and IoT, lead to a stress test of operational IP management.

In addition, digital patents are different. They do not come from physical reality or technical functionality, but from the application, the solution or the use case. These characteristics also affect analysis of the competitive situation, including taking third-party patents into account. A classic freedom-to-operate search, which has the purpose of identifying all relevant third-party patents largely to rule out infringement, is becoming so much more extensive and time-consuming that it sometimes looks as if it would be impossible. There are considerable dangers and liabilities lurking in the large patent portfolios of third parties, for example, when using mobile phone technologies for your own campus networks or IT technologies for new products.

Dealing with IP risks is not only one of the special challenges for entrepreneurs because of their possible impact on business operations, but also because of the personal consequences for managing directors and board members resulting from a violation of due diligence. These personal consequences can go as far as personal liability of the managing director. Such personal liability can occur, for example, if the management fails to take steps to prevent damage. Since failure to observe third-party IP rights can result in severe sanctions, such as sales bans or claims for damages, the identification and consideration of third-party patents is an essential element of damage prevention. Risk management not only raises the bar for internal IP management systems, but also when dealing with suppliers and partners.

Development of IP management standards

It is quite common for organizations to implement the ISO 9001:2015 quality management standard to improve their overall operational performance, establishing practices of continuous improvement and risk-based thinking. But as companies experience increasing IP challenges in the field of digital innovation, they need to adopt a more specific set-up to respond to the various threats they face. This leads to a new understanding of the use of standards in IP management as well.

IP management standards like ISO 56005[4] or DIN 77006[5] have been

3

created to support companies and IP service providers in developing their abilities to handle the challenges of a modern and compliant IP management. They provide guidance to the design of an up-to-date IP management system[6], ie, the introduction of effective processes and an allocation of tasks that are aligned with the company's strategy and business objectives. They focus on leadership and strategy, as well as tools and methods, such as the implementation of the concept 'plan-do-check-act'[7], as introduced in DIN 77006, which leads to improved productivity and error prevention[8].

Externally, expectations are rising as well. Before a larger organization partners with an SME or a high-tech growth business, it will often want to see an IP management standard in place, so offsetting any potential risks to itself.

ISO 56005: guidance to tools and methods for IP management

In 2014, the International Organization for Standardization (ISO) set up the ISO/Technical Commission 279, aiming to provide tools and methods using the holistic approach to innovation management, its implementation and its interaction with stakeholders. The commission's main objective was to standardize tools and methods dedicated to the field of innovation and in interaction with all actors in its management for industrial, environmental and social benefits.

The ISO 5600X family is designed as a framework in a standardized format to support innovation management procedures starting from the idea, via research and development, up to the creation of the IP and verified products or services.

ISO 56005 as a part of the 5600X family is designed as a guideline to systematically manage IP within the innovation environment. It supports the innovation process and provides an IP strategy that is aligned with the business strategy, and includes five major activities and outcomes to help organizations protect and maximize their best ideas:

- IP landscaping

- IP creation and acquisition

- IP portfolio

- IP commercialization

- IP risk management

The ISO 56005 standard can be used for any type of innovation activities and initiatives and is based on certain principles derived from the innovation management system, such as:

- realization of value for all relevant stakeholders;

- leadership that inspires and engages employees, and other interested parties, to generate, protect and leverage IP;

- alignment of the overall strategic direction for managing IP with an organization's business and innovation strategies;

- access to a diverse range of internal and external IP knowledge sources for the systematic development of its IP expertise;

- management of innovation uncertainty and risks from an IP perspective;

- generation, protection and leveraging of IP for long-term value creation based on shared values, beliefs and behaviours across the organization.

IP management responsibilities related to innovation should include, for example:

- defining innovation outputs that need to be protected as the organization's IP assets and the appropriate resources to manage this IP;

- monitoring IP in the public domain that is relevant as an input to innovation activities to avoid potential infringement of third-party rights, to identify potential infringements of the organization's IP, and to report risk and opportunities to interested parties;

- establishing awareness and providing training within the organization.

The annex of ISO 56005 gives an overview regarding tools and methods for:

- Invention record and disclosure

- IP generation, acquisition and maintenance

- IP search

- IP evaluation

- IP risk management

It is a best-practice collection of directions and strategies of how to manage IP systematically within the innovation environment that is especially helpful for SMEs.

DIN 77006: requirements for IP management systems

In 2016, the German Institute for Standardization (DIN) constituted a working committee to deal with the creation of standards and specifications in the area of 'quality in IP management'.

The German DIN standard can generally be seen as a more specific, stricter version of the ISO 56005. It takes a comprehensive approach to the organizational landscape of the company with a strong focus on processes and quality and provides a set of rules to implement an IP management system (see Figure 1). DIN 77006 is a systematic tool to establish, implement, and maintain an IP management system in almost every organization and for almost all types of business models.

ISO 56005	DIN 77006
Guidelines to **innovation management**	Requirements for an IP management system
Design framework for the use of IP in innovation management	Optimization of the **entire organization** through quality-assured handling of IP
Definition of IP strategies to support the overall organization strategy	Creation of an IP strategy to achieve a long-term business goal
Application of consistent **IP tools and methods** to support efficient IP management	Integration of IP management into the company's management system
Best-practice recommendation	Auditable proof of conformity

Figure 1: Development of standards for IP management

If an organization already operates a single management system (eg, only quality) or an integrated management system (eg, quality and environment), it may additionally map the IP requirements of DIN 77006 without having to introduce a completely new system.

If no management system exists yet, DIN 77006 contains all the essential requirements to establish an IP management system that is based on internationally accepted standards.

An important aspect of the compatibility of management systems is the uniform standard structure, HLS or High Level Structure[9]. According to this structure, the organization can combine different requirements and create an integrated management system (IMS)[10], for example, ISO 9001 plus DIN 77006 or ISO 9001 and ISO 14001[11] plus DIN 77006.

According to this common structure, any organization can integrate its identified and documented IP processes into an existing, known and established management system structure. DIN 77006 is fully compatible with the general HLS standard requirements, eg, context and interested parties, leadership, risk and opportunity management, planning of goals and many more requirements like internal audits, management reviews and improvement[12].

Process model

What the standards of the ISO 9001 family have in common is a process model that establishes a cycle of plan-do-check-act (PDCA)[13] within the company. This cycle receives impetus from customer demands and feedback from expressions of customer satisfaction or dissatisfaction. It serves to make constant improvements to the quality management system[14].

The process model assumes that the phases of the improvement cycle consist of processes that are interconnected[15]. The processes for creating products and providing services are triggered by customer requirements and end with a service to the customer. They are designed and enabled by management and resource processes. Supporting processes (eg, development, procurement, accounting) provide services to the core processes or to external interested parties who are not customers.

The purpose of an IP management system from a business perspective is to provide an organizational framework to deal with IP risks and opportunities among other things. The IP management system is established as an iterative process:

- IP strategy and policy are generated, published and communicated.

- IP risks and IP opportunities are to be determined and appropriate IP objectives and processes are to be defined (plan).

- The corresponding processes are then to be carried out as part of operation or support (do). They concern the topics of IP awareness, administration, generation, enforcement, defence and transactions (do).

- The performance and effectiveness of the IP management system must be checked regularly and recorded using IP reporting (check), the IP management system must be evaluated by internal or external audits systematically. The results are documented as a management system review.

- Improvements to the IP management system are subsequently initiated (act), if necessary.

The standard explicitly points out that IP management must be aligned with the overall strategy of the company, but that the above processes can be carried out both within the company and externally, ie, by third parties. Accordingly, suitable agreements must be made with these service providers to ensure compliance with standards.

DIN 77006 helps an organization establish an efficient and legally secure IP management system. The systematic approach of DIN 77006 (PDCA principle) with the documentation requirements across all hierarchical levels and processes ensures that all relevant legal and regulatory requirements can be met and that processes are optimally integrated in terms of achieving corporate goals.

The introduction of DIN 77006 provides benefits for industrial companies and service providers in the IP sector:

- by providing a comprehensive and practical set of rules;

- through the integration of IP (partial) processes into the core processes of the company;

- by creating the necessary conditions to increase opportunities in the development of patentable (digital) business models and use cases;

- through the introduction of risk management for IP and thus the reduction of possible liability risks;

- and last, but not least, by communicating IP's contemporary role to internal and external employees responsible both for IP and for the future of the company.

By establishing, implementing and maintaining an IP management system compliant with DIN 77006, a company will be able to meet the diverse challenges of the upcoming digital transformation more securely and efficiently.

• *The full version of this article first appeared in the September 2022 edition of les Nouvelles, the journal of the Licensing Executives Society under the title 'Standards for the quality of IP management' and is available at: www. epo.org/learning/materials/sme/high-growth-technology-businesses/ip-professionals.html*

CEIPI is the Centre of Intellectual Property Studies at the University of Strasbourg. The authors of its review of IP standards were Alexander J. Wurzer, Jamie Soon-Kesteloot, Bastian Best, Nicky Wennemer, Martin Wilming, Sven Calsbach, Wolfgang Berres, Stephan Wolke, Hanns-Peter Tümmler, Axel Mittelstaedt, Lorenz Kaiser, Tobias Denk and Theo Grünewald.

Notes

[1.] This article is based on a German publication, *DIN 77006: Ein Managementsystem für den Umgang mit IP*, Wolfgang Berres et al, *Mitteilungen der deutschen Patentanwälte*, 112 no.11 (November 2021) 473 – 524

[2.] Emiliano Sisinni et al, Internet of Things: Challenges, Opportunities, and Directions, IEEE Transactions on Industrial Informatics, 14 (November 2018) 4724-4734

[3.] Moore James F., Predators and Prey: The New Ecology of Competition, Harvard Business Review, 71 (1993) 75-83

[4.] ISO 56005:2020-11, *Innovation management - Tools and methods for intellectual property management - Guidance*

[5.] DIN 77006:2020-06, *Intellectual property management systems – Requirements*

[6.] Axel Mittelstaedt, *Strategisches IP-Management – mehr als nur Patente*, Wiesbaden: 2009, 55ff; Alexander J. Wurzer, Theo Grünewald and Wolfgang Berres, *Die 360° IP-Strategie*, München:

2016, 187ff; Oliver Gassmann, Martin A. Bader and Mark James Thompson, *Patent Management*, Cham: 2021, 103ff

[7.] Abhijit Chakraborty, *Importance of PDCA Cycle for SMEs*, SSRG International Journal of Mechanical Engineering, 3 (May 2016) 13-17

[8.] Alexander J. Wurzer, Stephan Hundertmark, *IP Management – Key Skills in a Knowledge Economy*, Journal of Korean Law, 8 (December 2008) 181-200

[9.] Peter Mendel, *The Making and Expansion of International Management Standards: The Global Diffusion of ISO 9000 Quality Management Certificates*, in: Gili S. Dorori, John W. Meyer and Hokyu Hwang, *Globalization and Organization*, Oxford: 2006, 137ff

[10.] M Asif, Erik J. De Bruijn and Olaf A. M. Fischer, *Corporate motivation for integrated management system Implementation: Why do firms engage in integration of management systems: A literature review and research agenda*, in: 16th Annual High Technology Small Firms Conference, HTSF 2008, Enschede, the Netherlands.

[11.] ISO 14001:2015, *Environmental management systems – Requirements with guidance for use*

[12.] Agota Giedre Raisiene, *Advantages and Limitations of Integrated Management System*, The Theoretical Viewpoint, 1 no1 (2011) 25-36

[13.] Mary Walton, *The Deming management method*, New York, 1986

[14.] Michael Bell and Vincent Omachonu, *Quality system implementation process for business success*, International Journal of Quality & Reliability Management, 28 no.7 (August 2011) 723-734

[15.] Milé Terziovski and Jose-Luis Guerrero, *ISO9000 quality system certification and its impact on product and process innovation performance*, International Journal of Production Economics, 158 (December 2014) 197-207

2.

IP STARTS UP GREEK REVIVAL

Economies, careers and lives are transformed, when intellectual property gives ventures the potential to scale, says Dimitris Kouzelis, a former EPO director, now the founder of Intellex

A decade ago Greece was bust. The prospect of it becoming a tech hub and home to dynamic start-ups seemed remote when the economy was locked into a spiral of austerity.

Those gloomy assumptions are now being dispelled. Greece is becoming one of the European Union's fastest growing economies, creating an ecosystem for tech and opening the way for IP ventures to scale. Its first unicorns are emerging (start-ups with a value of over $1 billion) and a record $500 million went into backing early-stage ventures in 2021.

Many of these are based in Athens where a large innovation centre is opening at an abandoned chemical factory. Several universities and research institutions, including the National Technical University of Athens and the Demokritos Research Institute, are creating incubators for technology spin-offs. Several of these ventures have a strong US or UK influence. Among them are potential unicorns, such as Accusonus, Viva Wallet and Softmotive, although most of their development takes place in Greece.

For talent, such ventures are drawing heavily on the young Greek diaspora, who despaired of their country after the financial crisis of 2008 and left to pursue international careers. They are now ready to return and apply the lessons they have learnt about managing innovation and growth. Greece has taken a lead too in attracting digital nomads, pioneering an attractive tax regime for those who can run a business from anywhere.

Mobile robotics

Many of these pieces came together for Myrmex, in which Ocado, the UK online retailer, bought a minority stake in 2020. It was originally set up in the US by two Greek engineers, Ioannis Kanellos and Eugenios Fainekos, to develop mobile robotics for the last point in the chain of home shopping.

At collection points, orders are automatically moved in their bins to the delivery truck or to a waiting customer. Frustrating waits are eliminated and pick-ups can be made at any time, day or night. The experience is designed to be like going to an ATM.

Patents on the technology were originally filed in the United States, whilst new applications are being made at the European Patent Office. All of Myrmex's research and development take places in Athens.

IP capabilities

Ventures like Myrmex are making it an exciting time for the Greek economy, says Dimitris Kouzelis, who is taking a lead in building up

IP capabilities both in Greece and in the wider eastern Mediterranean. Originally, he was a research scientist himself, who after his first degree at home, studied in Paris, developing a laser measuring system for aero jet engines. Kouzelis never convinced his superiors to patent it, as they preferred to publish the results in line with academic expectations at the time.

So, instead of creating a spin-off, he joined the European Patent Office, first as an examiner and then as a director. Four years ago, he left to set up his own IP practice to support a revival based on the energy and talent of young Greeks. It is a task that he fears might be undermined by cultural reservations, institutional frailties and professional shortages.

Cultural reservations

Traditionally, Greek innovators relied on two basic forms of IP: the improvised draft or poor man's protection. In the first case, they would draft their own patent descriptions or ask a friendly lawyer to help. They might well be able to write an adequate technical description, but claims require a fine balance between technical accuracy and legal scope. The unfortunate consequence was that the details of an innovation were frequently disclosed without a strong enough defence, so others were free to develop it.

The alternative for disillusioned Greeks was to tell no one about an idea and keep it a secret: the so-called poor man's protection. The trouble is that it excludes you from the investment and support on which you will rely to grow the idea. Without protection, ideas are now almost instantly shared anyway. Those with more experience and finance then bring them to market.

Costs and benefits

The international experience of the Greek diaspora and the emergence of ventures such as Myrmex and Accusonus is encouraging a new generation of innovators to think again about the economics of investing in patents.

Broadly, the cost of an initial application will be less than €5000. Then it will take another €5000 to file an international application for 30/31 months under the Patent Co-operation Treaty. At the national phase, when you chose where to file, it typically costs €35,000 for ten markets and examination fees could amount to the same.

These costs will be phased, of course, and at each stage the value of an innovation will rise. As an application, an innovation has a relatively low value. Once it receives a positive search report from an examiner, it value will rise by two, four or eight times.

So, at each stage, innovators can talk to investors about funding the next round. In Greece, a system is establishing itself where these conversations can take place, not least because the owners of traditional industries, such as shipping, are actively seeking to diversify and transform their own performance by investing in tech.

Institutional failings

The EU's introduction of a unitary patent and a unified patent court represent a triumph for streamlining this process. From 2022, a single patent within a single jurisdiction will apply in 25 European countries.

Unfortunately, Greece is ill equipped to benefit. Like many countries in south-east Europe, it has yet to ratify the unitary patent and it hasn't waived the requirement for a local translation under the London Agreement.

Its other shortcoming is a lack of European patent attorneys, upon whom the smooth working of the system depends. Greece has six in total, most of who are part time. For Greek innovators, the usual option is to turn to professionals in leading tech locations, such as the US or Germany. Realistically, they cannot expect to rely on being given as much priority as if they were a local champion.

Lasting impact

In his regular talks to graduates around the eastern Mediterranean, Dimitris Kouzelis explains the role that patents are playing in the resurgence of economies like Greece. Their use by US joint ventures and the returning diaspora is now having a real economic and psychological impact, he says.

However, if talk of unicorns is to take on real substance, it depends on bringing the IP system up to speed. As Greece and the eastern Mediterranean transform themselves, he tells his audiences of researchers and scientists, a career as a patent attorney is one to consider seriously, both for themselves and for the resurgence of the region's economies.

Dimitris Kouzelis is a former director of the European Patent Office and founder of Intellex, a pioneer in giving advice on IP strategies to start-ups, SMEs and research labs in Greece and the eastern Mediterranean. Further details at: www.intel-lex.eu.

3.
DEEP TECH TO MARKET

High growth, high impact? Four EPO case studies highlight the IP experiences and insights gained through adapting early-stage, high-risk technologies for everyday use. Thomas Bereuter and Ilja Rudyk report

Giving e-bikes the brakes to match their speed. Connecting wind turbines to the internet of things. Creating more freedom to design for 3D printers. Taking augmented reality into the operating theatre.

All involve the adaptation of deep tech. It's a daunting task to turn such complex breakthroughs in technology into applications that can be used at scale. Most early-stage technical solutions can't simply be licensed or brought to market. Intensive work is required in terms of their design, engineering and approval. Supply chains have to be created, entry barriers to the market overcome and regulatory tests passed.

Spin-outs of research organisations lay the groundwork for commercializing such early-stage, high-risk technologies. They create a clear framework for developing intellectual property as a technology advances or for following up a unique sales proposition in a market that is yet to be developed. Often run by ambitious postgraduates, they combine an understanding of the underlying science with the adoption of an industrial and commercial mindset, often facilitated by partners.

For seed investors or funders, a spin-out's package of IP acts as a main guarantee for taking the technology to a stage where it can appeal to a more mainstream financial audience without the risk of copycats taking over.

In a new series of case studies from the European Patent Office, four ventures in deep tech have shared the challenges they have overcome in reaching the market and highlighted the lessons they have learnt in transforming research for use in real life.

The rewards for resolving such challenges can be both high impact and high growth. Most accidents on e-bikes happen when braking. In an energy crisis, it is best to minimize the damage that ice and lightning cause to wind turbines. 3D printing took its time to embrace alternative materials and widen its application range to everyone. An ageing society benefits if knee replacements don't require follow-up surgery to put them right.

Smarter by design and co-operation

Four million Europeans are now buying e-bikes a year, even if safety remains a concern. Most accidents happen when braking. What if anti-locking technology could be transferred from motor sports? This was the inspiration for a spin-out from one of Europe's largest technical schools, Polimi (Politechnico di Milano), in collaboration with an incubator of deep-tech companies, e-Novia.

Their common goal was to use the next generation of artificial intelligence to create an open system for the design of braking systems that could be fitted inside the frame of each manufacturer's e-bike. Riders would then experience better traction and better balance when caught out by the speed or the weight of their e-bike.

It's an ambitious and complex structure for upgrading how e-bikes are made, which relies on IP that is secure enough to break into the market and flexible enough for partnerships with manufacturers. Polimi secured the rights to the anti-locking technology and licensed them to the spin-out it created with e-Novia in 2015, Blubrake, whose first product appeared in 2021 after six years of further research and development.

Unusually, Blubrake took its time to file any patents of its own, initially preferring to operate under confidentiality. Its policy is to protect technology for close-to-market applications and manage its IP in close step with its technology road map.

Blubrake differentiates itself by co-designing solutions with e-bike manufacturers, as opposed to the proprietary models that its competitors offer. As a supplier, it would risk losing the value of such partnerships without the close management of the IP it has developed. On the basis of this balanced model, Blubrake raised €5.2m in 2021 to fund the next stage of its growth.

From platform to focus and exit

An early exploration by five entrepreneurial postgraduates into the potential for adopting optical sensors as a platform technology for industries such as rail, space and medical led to the creation of a more tightly focused spin-out, fos4X, in 2012.

One of the advantages of operating under the umbrella of a university such as TUM (Technical University of Munich) is that it has the reach to generate early feedback about where demand really lies. In a response to a press release about the progress of their work, some of Germany's leading industrial players identified wind turbines as the most pressing challenge that optical sensors could solve.

Fos4X switched its focus to finding a better solution to managing the millions of load switches that a wind turbine will experience in its lifetime. The electrical sensors that were being used struggled to respond in adverse conditions, such as lightning and ice. Fos4X's combination of light sensors and smart materials promised more resilience and accuracy.

The founders were well prepared to break into the market: TUM encourages its postgraduates to think about the potential for starting a company during their research and treats patents as a currency of equal value to publications. The supervising professor is even a European patent attorney and has experience with a total of six spin-outs.

On this basis, fos4X was able to build a case for four years of funding before making its first significant sale. Although it started under an exclusive licence from TUM, it exercised an option to buy all related IP in 2018.

By 2020, when fos4X was acquired by Polytech, a Danish manufacturer of products and services for the wind industry, its sales had reached €11 million and it had a portfolio of 200 patents in 80 patent families. Its capabilities in IP and innovation were one of its main attractions as an acquisition target: the fos4X managers responsible are now occupying similar roles for all of Polytech.

Usage rights for multiple innovation paths

Two spin-outs are gaining scale within a cluster of 3D printing companies around the Technical University of Vienna. The origin of these two ventures lies in a series of questions that Professor Jürgen Stampfl started asking in 3D printing's early days as a technology in the 2000s. In particular, could its use be extended more creatively to other materials, notably ceramics and then industrial polymers?

First, he had to team up with colleagues in chemistry to develop the materials and then find an industrial partner to further explore a novel use of machinery for 3D printing. He formed a partnership with Ivoclar, a dental specialist, which continues to flourish today.

Together, they have created 20 patent families which they jointly own. Ivoclar has kept all the rights for dental applications, covers the cost of any research not publicly funded and pays the IP bills. TU Vienna retains all the other usage rights and shares the royalties with Ivoclar.

The two spin-outs that have evolved from this platform are partly managed by postgraduates and Professor Stampfl. Lithoz, which prints 3D ceramics for biomedical and industrial applications, now employs 110 people. A more recent spin-out, Cubicure, is working on innovations in 3D printing for industrial polymers. Each spin-out operates under a separate set of licences for materials and machines from TU Vienna, although both have started to file their own patents, continuing the cycle of innovation that began at the university.

'It's appealing for our students to have the chance to apply research in an industrial setting,' says Professor Stampfl. 'Such partnerships depend on recognizing the value of an industrial mindset. You have to step back from being an innovator and recognize that it's not easy to raise money, manage safety or hire people. So in the beginning, it's about innovation. Later on, it's about implementation and operation.'

'We want to give our industrial partners all the rights they require and retain all the other rights, so we don't cut off future developments and we can work with other partners.'

Disruption in the operating theatre

Letting surgeons track the progress of their operations on their mobiles: it's an approach that is about to take hip and knee replacements to a new level of reliability. Ten years ago, however, few in medical imaging were giving much thought to the potential of augmented reality (AR). Operating theatres remained their own safely contained, expensively fitted world.

An entrepreneurial professor at the University of Coimbra in Portugal, João Barreto, took a more disruptive view. He and a research student, Rui Melo, started investigating image processing for keyhole surgery.

What if you could remove any distortions in the video feeds to give surgeons a more accurate view and then overlay clinical information on their screens? Through AR, they realized they could create a navigation system for surgeons that bypassed much of the existing infrastructure on which operating theatres relied.

At the time, such thinking was seen by established companies as too early and too high risk to license. So in 2013, a spin-out, Perceive3D (P3D), was created with seed funding from a public agency, Portugal Ventures. A clear line was drawn with the university regarding IP. P3D gained an exclusive licence to the technology, assumed responsibility for all IP costs and agreed to pay royalties to a set limit.

In markets as competitive as medical imaging, patents often represent the best chance of breaking in. As P3D was developing a technology from scratch, its policy was to 'patent the roots not the branches'. Its aim was to cover a broader scope of applications with fewer patents.

For now, P3D's focus is on the market for keyhole and open surgery. Its IP allows it to pursue a twin-track business model, licensing its technology in some fields and developing applications in its own niches. In 2022, it released its navigation system for hip surgery in partnership with a leading implant manufacturer. In parallel, it is launching its own branded product for knees.

Unusually, the founders have involved themselves in drafting the patent claims, both to give themselves room to diversify and to retain any future value for investors. Ultimately, their vision is to bring AR to all of surgery and open up the potential for many more applications.

Pointers for high-growth IP

Each of these case studies draws on the insights and experiences of multiple actors involved in adapting research for real-world uses. Taken together, they form a series of IP pointers that matter most along the path to high growth. These options and lessons emerge in full in each of the EPO's case studies. Here are some of the highlights.

- Put ventures in the hands of ambitious postgraduates and create an ecosystem of support to get those ventures off the ground.

- Encourage researchers to treat publications and patents as twin currencies of comparable value.

- When developing a platform technology from scratch, retain the core IP to create the potential for further spin-outs.

- When commercializing an early-stage technology, first operate under confidentiality, then line up the IP in close-to-market applications.

- Licensing works well when a technology is ready for the market; spin-outs are a better option when more proof and advancement is required.

- Patents create a sustainable point of entry to established markets dominated by major players.

- Create a clear IP framework between universities, research partners and spin-outs that allows for an ongoing partnership and a clear regulation of ownership and use rights for investors.

- Recognise the balance between innovation and implementation. Universities work in three-year cycles exploring the new; industrial partners accumulate decades of experience and practical know-how.

- IP is instrumental to the financial fate of a spin-out at two particular points: when lining up a continuous stream of investment, particularly in the early stages, and when determining an exit value in the event of a trade sale or flotation.

- To ingrain an active sense of IP as an asset, encourage spin-outs to draft their own patent descriptions and brainstorm about potential claims, before having them revised and completed professionally.

- An active IP culture encourages the early disclosure of inventions and forestalls the risk of losing novelty and inventive steps to incremental publications and other disclosures.

- Design platform IP to allow the option of pursuing two business models. You can then license your tech to different industries while exploring your own niche applications.

- Keep IP protection in step with your technology road map, so you develop the ability to keep capturing new sources of innovation and value.

For the full versions of the case studies that the EPO has published about high-growth, high-impact technology transfer, see: epo.org/case-studies.

Thomas Bereuter is innovation support programme area manager at the European Patent Academy of the European Patent Office in Munich. **Ilja Rudyk** is senior economist at the European Patent Office in Munich.

4.
READY TO COLLABORATE
WITH INTELLECTUAL ASSETS

Collaborations let you accelerate, but their results can be unpredictable if you're not clear on the status of your intellectual assets, says Ia Modin at Westerberg & Partners

The speed at which markets are now developing compels companies to make use of all accessible inputs to keep themselves relevant to their customers. At the same time, an ever-growing part of a company's value lies in its intellectual assets (IAs), which makes all sharing of information in collaborations a high-risk practice. Collaborations can range from engaging with a consultant or supplier to improve an existing product, to participating in large, publicly funded research consortia or joining forces with academics in solving specific challenges.

A company that knows the detail and nature of the information that it possesses is in a significantly better position to protect its trade secrets and to commercialize its innovations. To understand its portfolio of IAs and to have a foundation for strategic decisions, it will make and maintain an inventory of these assets.

To limit risks and make sure that use of results will be unrestricted, contractual decision-making for every collaboration will be active and strategic, rather than random or arbitrary. The basis of such decisions is a strategic understanding of the IAs in relation to the business model and the specific collaboration that the agreement is set to govern. By aligning business strategy with IAs, a company can respond to any challenges and opportunities in a way which will maximize commercialization and returns on investment.

Identifying and understanding intellectual assets

Inventory

An inventory compiles the IAs which have been identified and listed, itemizing them into their smallest units and documenting their characteristics, attributes and properties together with additional relevant information. It can be made and managed using a detailed spreadsheet or specialized software. Growing numbers of managers now use blockchain. It is best to limit access to the inventory to as few individuals within the company as possible.

A challenge to compiling the inventory is seeing the information with new eyes. Our brains are developed to disregard well-known patterns which makes separating and itemizing familiar details difficult to most people. A good starting point can be your registered intellectual property rights, but don't stop at this point. Even a patent may comprise numerous assets, such as knowledge on separate applications, rights granted for different territories, associated items of know-how, as well as information not disclosed in the patent applications, such as plans for future development work and notes on what did not work.

There will also be many IAs which at first glance only seem to be snippets, but when inspected prove to be more significant. For companies, heavily engaged in research and development, a large proportion of IAs consist of negative information, knowing what does not work.

It is better to avoid grouping assets under the typical headlines such as trade secrets, copyright and inventions, as it risks blurring the fact that certain information assets may be attributed to several different categories. It may well prove to be beneficial at a later stage if you keep them open. A decision to patent, for example, needs to be preceded by an active decision based on an assessment of whether to make the information public or keep it confidential. An item in a category named 'invention' may cause you to neglect this assessment. 'Trade secrets' is also a headline to avoid as the variety of information in such a group will make it impractical.

Additional information for each asset in the inventory may include the time of latest update, its relation to other assets and a note on its estimated monetary value (considering, for example, the costs to a competitor to obtain, acquire or develop it or the potential licence fee).

Strategic tool

To further ensure additional practical use of the inventory as a basis for strategy, additional relevant categories should be included, such as technology readiness level (TRL), maturity of the information, need for development efforts, protectability under IP laws, estimated value to competitors and need for confidentiality.

A category of particular importance is value. Either assign a relative value on any given scale (1–5 or 1–100) to show each asset's relative position compared to other assets; or estimate a monetary value, considering, for example, the costs of a competitor to obtain, acquire or develop the information or the potential licence revenue. An asset scoring in the top on 'value to our competitors', as well as 'importance/relevance to our business/products' and 'need to keep confidential', while low on 'protectability under IP laws', must be kept in strict confidence with restricted internal access and with high thresholds to divulging the information to any third party, even under any non-disclosure agreement (NDA).

An asset scoring low on 'importance/relevance to our business/ products' while receiving top scores for both TRL, maturity of information and IP protectability will be easily identified as an asset to sell or license out. Alternatively, it can highlight where to explore new business outside your core.

The information in the inventory may also be used to plot the items in a diagram enabling schematic overviews of certain assets, visualizing and identifying clusters of assets having similar properties. For consistency the x-axis may be reserved for 'importance/relevance to our business/products' while the y-axis alternates between the other categories, creating different visual representations of the assets.

Trade secrets

Many, even most, IAs are held as trade secrets. In fact, most products, services and even inventions started as a piece of information held as a trade secret. A trade secret is defined as commercially valuable information which a company keeps confidential and has value in not being known to others.

For the trade secret to enjoy legal protection, most jurisdictions require reasonable steps to have been taken to ensure that it remains confidential. Such steps vary with information and circumstance, but include identifying, documenting and applying physical, technical and legal means and measures to ensure confidentiality.

As a trade secret's protection is destroyed by disclosure, keeping the information confidential is crucial. From a practical point of view, proving or even knowing that a valuable trade secret has been divulged or used without permission is often difficult and the calculation of potential damage even harder. So it is crucial to contractually require third parties who gain access to your information to proactively protect its confidentiality.

In most cases of information sharing with a collaborating party, an NDA with relevant provisions is best put in place. When the information you are sharing includes trade secrets, you will be looking to ensure legal protection too.

Recipients who are contractually bound to establish concrete measures and document their handling of a trade secret have been shown to greatly improve their information management. The greater the importance and value of what you are sharing, the greater the effort to stipulate and specify measures to be undertaken by the recipient, as well as the details on the specific use allowed. Remember that for the most sensitive trade secrets, access to third parties should be as limited as possible.

Assigning responsibility

Protecting information, especially trade secrets, needs a solid internal strategy and set of best practices. Assigning responsibility for the strategic management of specific assets, especially those to be kept confidential, to named persons (rather than units or departments), and to have this information set out in a separate category in the inventory, will greatly increase your standards of IA management.

Identify and assign gatekeepers for sensitive and valuable information, who are engaged in managing the asset and maintaining secrecy. They will keep track of any sharing of this information with third parties and the NDAs signed, as well as knowing if the information has become obsolete, lost its value or become a matter of general knowledge. As IAs are constantly evolving, the inventory must be kept up to date and relevant.

Collaborations

The potential for companies to collaborate is wide, so choose wisely, both when it comes to where to put your efforts and how to protect shared IAs.

Needs-driven collaborations

Engaging in strategically driven collaborations, guided by and addressing core needs and challenges for the business, present or future, is vital. Using your inventory, you can identify areas for complementary and supporting development. Assessing assets scoring high on either 'importance/relevance to our business/products' or 'relevance to our next generation product/services', while scoring low for TRL and maturity of information gives you a good starting point for identifying areas of where to make a collaborative effort.

For collaborations that address the needs of your company, you will have to accept some risk exposure. To achieve commercially valuable results, relevant IAs and information about your needs (which in itself may be highly sensitive information) must be contributed. As results are expected from the collaboration, it will be essential to ensure you will have full freedom to operate in making use of them and perhaps even keep them as a trade secret (solely or jointly with other participants).

For these kinds of collaboration, you can expect to invest in drafting and negotiating full and optimal provisions regarding at least background information, confidentiality and results.

Explorative collaborations

Companies may also choose to participate in a large array of explorative collaborations, which are not expected to respond to identified needs of your present or future business. Such collaborations can be outside the company's core business, have an academic focus or have a low TRL.

All such endeavours may be approved by the company, providing it has the time, energy and finances to support it. However, when upsides are unclear, risks must be kept low. Therefore, sensitive assets can be protected by being kept out of such collaborations, possibly with the exemption of easily enforced registered rights, which may already be widely licensed. Assets scoring high in the category 'need to keep confidential', 'importance/relevance to our business/products' and 'value to our competitors' must not be contributed, regardless of the confidentiality provisions of the collaboration agreement.

As there are no identified expectations of specific outcomes of these collaborations, the agreement will likely not need to include pre-negotiated usage rights to results and an option to a licence on commercial terms could be acceptable. When neither contributing nor receiving sensitive information, and without demanding pre-negotiated usage rights to results, contractual transaction costs can be kept to a minimum.

Collaboration agreements

From a legal perspective, it is always best to ensure the correct and optimal contractual governance for collaborations, including provisions on background information, confidentiality and results, to protect your information and to secure your future freedom to operate. In practice, smaller companies cannot keep up, internal support may be insufficient and external legal support is too costly to entrust with every case.

In addition to the cost aspect, the parties have often already initiated the collaboration, leading both sides to want to focus on affirmations and positive aspects, avoiding matters on which they may potentially disagree. It is often also true for large companies.

Legal departments are surprisingly often considered by internal R&D units to be a bottleneck. Some even consider their work to be a 'necessary corporate evil' that must be kept from delaying or causing obstacles to the real work of the project. Such factors combined seem to fuel internal R&D units to bypass the legal department and get started with the collaboration. It is probably caused by a lack of understanding of the commercial and strategic benefits that contractual strategic work may bring to the business both in terms of mitigating risks and facilitating commercialization.

Many companies accept standard, readily available template collaboration agreements, regardless of the demands of each case. These templates are usually complex and typically quite detailed as regards certain provisions, such as access rights to background information and results. To use them for governing collaborations where little sensitive information is shared and outputs are of comparatively low TRL or of low commercial value causes unnecessary obstacles and costs.

However, the same standard templates are often quite inadequate for collaborations where sensitive and confidential information is shared and outputs are expected to be significant and valuable. Typically, they are lacking in detailed and practical provisions regarding essential matters such as co-ownership of results and the confidentiality of trade secrets. Companies would wisely choose when to reject the standard templates and instead strategically invest in negotiating optimal and unambiguous provisions being relevant for the collaboration at hand.

Ia Modin is a partner at Westerberg & Partners, a Swedish boutique law firm that focuses on IP law and commercial disputes. She is a specialist in intellectual assets, patents, copyright and trade secrets. She has extensive experience of complex multi-party agreements related to future IP rights, such as R&D, art, music and film. She works primarily as a legal facilitator of innovation, collaboration and commercialization with a view to finding optimal win-win solutions.

5.
FOUR TECHNOLOGY
LICENSING BUSINESS MODELS

Bowman Heiden and Thomas Bereuter discuss how high-growth technology businesses can model their licensing options to maximize the potential for revenue and impact

Why license? Well, there are many reasons. Fundamentally, licensing is a way of providing access to technology in exchange for money or other benefits, such as access to other technology (known as cross-licensing[1]). Rather than assigning technology to a buyer at an agreed price, licensing allows parties to share success and risk and, in most cases, to avoid having to put a price on the technology, which, in the early stages of its development, is often problematic[2]. Due to globalization and the increasing complexity and convergence of technology, companies are pushed to rely more on open innovation – which includes greater collaboration with external partners to gain access to technology – and to commercialize their technology broadly, thereby sharing success and risk by pooling assets that are required to successfully launch new products and services[3].

This is particularly important for enabling technologies that have many applications across different markets. Thus, it is possible to set up a business model which is built entirely on licensing or, more typically, a business model that combines licensing with the licensor's own research, development and production. In this way, a company may be open to licensing in certain areas and within a certain scope, while also directly commercializing part of the technology itself.

Two interfaces

It is important for technology companies to understand how they can use licensing to improve both the development and commercialization of their technologies:

Development

Development includes partners and co-opetitors[4] through whom the licensor seeks to gain access to the technology it needs to develop its value proposition. In general, licensing for development/access serves to reduce the cost and increase the speed of development, or to reduce the legal risk for the company via enhanced freedom to operate (FTO).

Commercialization

This includes the vertical and horizontal partners that will further commercialize the licensor's technology across the main vertical applications and markets, as well as other complementary applications and markets horizontally. In general, licensing for commercialization can help companies generate revenue in areas where direct participation on the market for the product or service concerned is a challenge (eg,

37

due to high-entry barriers). It also provides a solution for companies that just do not have the capacity to pursue all available options.

Four business models

Figure 1 below provides a simple framework of basic licence-based business models for high-growth technology businesses. It presents the four relationships available to technology companies on the technology market within its two main interfaces.

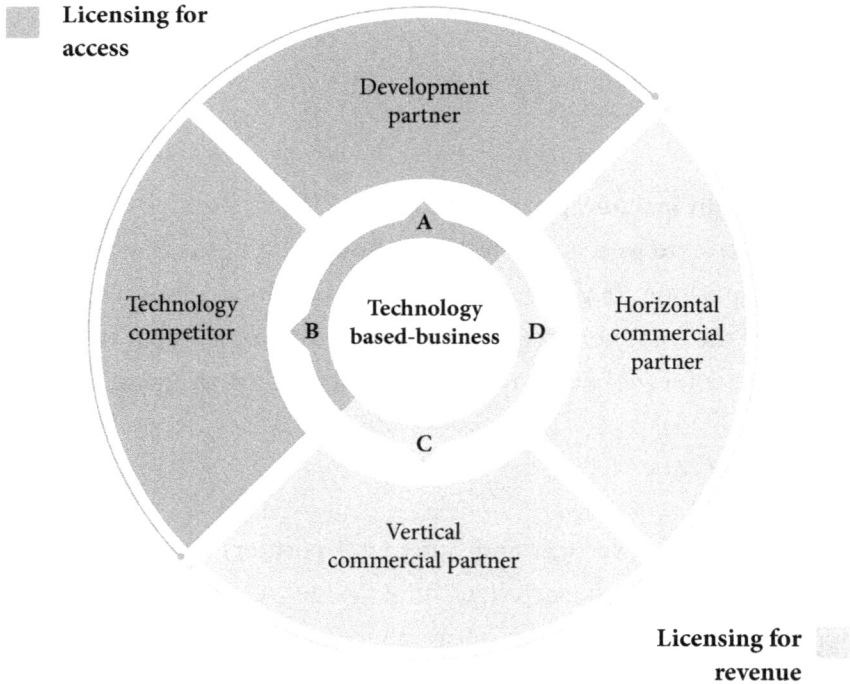

Licensing for access

Development partner

A

Technology competitor   B   Technology based-business   D   Horizontal commercial partner

C

Vertical commercial partner

Licensing for revenue

Figure 1. Licence-based business models for technology companies

A) Access to technology from a development partner

In this licensing model, the licensor works with development partners to gain access to key technology resources and/or capabilities that are not present within its own business or are too time-consuming, costly, difficult or risky to develop internally. Licensing in necessary technologies can help to reduce costs, reduce lead times and enhance value propositions. This type of licensing is also a primary technology transfer method for university-based start-ups, which often license in IP from their source institutions. There are various technology transfer case studies[5] that focus on this particular aspect. Two examples are the university spin-outs Cubicure (Austria), an additive manufacturing company, and Blubrake (Italy), which develops an anti-lock braking system (ABS) for e-bikes[6].

B) Freedom to operate from a potential competitor

In this licensing model, the licensor seeks to gain access to the IP of potential competitors. Instead of accessing technology, the focus of an FTO business agreement is typically on licensing IP rights (eg, patents) to mitigate the risk of infringement or in response to a threat of invalidation of the company's own patents. This is typically a contentious agreement resulting in the exchange of money and/or the mutual cross-licensing of IP rights. If the licence also delivers access to technology resources or knowledge, see model A; if it results in a net payment to the technology company, see model D. For an example of how a de facto cross-licensing agreement secured freedom to operate, see the case study on French digital communication company Webdyn[7].

C) Vertical commercial partner: licensing vs production

In this licensing model, the licensor seeks to commercialize technology as a primary means of generating revenue in full or in part. The technology company could license its technology exclusively to one other company in return for royalties on the sale of products/services utilizing the technology – a model typical of the life sciences industry. For an example, see the case study on Dermis Pharma, a Turkish company that develops medical products[8]. Other options include granting non-exclusive licences to multiple actors within the same market, as is typical in ICT (a strategy applied, for example, by Spanish telecommunication technology provider Fractus[9]) or granting an exclusive licence to specific actors across different geographies, as many SMEs do, or a specific field of use in the case of platform technologies. This licensing model can be combined with a technology company's own direct commercialization on some markets and licensing on others (ie, a hybrid approach), as practised by the Austrian biotech company Marinomed[10]. Note that the sale of technology components or materials to downstream actors can also benefit from technology licensing covering usage, rights to further development and associated trade marks.

D) Horizontal commercial partner: complementary licensing

This model is similar to model C but focuses on generating revenue as a secondary means of commercializing a technology. This can include the licensing of technologies that are non-core to the company or in fields of use that are beyond its projected commercial roadmap. See, for example, the strategy of Swedish technical textiles developer and provider Oxeon[11]. This model can be useful as a means of generating revenue to support growth or for providing proof-of-concept evidence for use on other markets. As an alternative to licensing, a company can also sell non-core IP. For an example, see the case study of German company fos4X[12].

IP transfers

It is important to clearly define the licensed object, ie, formulate exactly to what the licensee obtains access. From a technology perspective, the licensed object may primarily consist of a patent or a patent application (in full or in part) and technical know-how not included in the patent or patent application. Additionally, the licensed object may consist of copyrights, software, databases, design rights, trade marks, biological materials etc.

The licensed object should be matched to the technology and market situation. It is not at all self-evident that a company should license its entire patent portfolio, or even an entire patent family, so these decisions require serious thought. For example, if one patent from a package is not technologically relevant for the licensee, it does not make much sense to provide access to it. Nor is it necessarily a good idea to grant a licence to patents covering geographical markets where the licensee does not have any kind of activity. However, know-how is less bound to specific geographical areas.

Patents and patent applications are fairly easy to refer to, since they have official numbers that may be cited. Know-how is more difficult to cover in the form of a patent claim. In our experience, there are two main ways of handling know-how: make a list of documents containing know-how in an appendix or define know-how by reference to its subject matter. For example, all know-how necessary to optimize the technology package. This should ideally involve collaboration between

41

a technical expert and a lawyer. Also note that while the licensee might well be able to create the know-how itself, it is often more cost and time efficient to obtain a licence, enabling both companies to benefit from the research already done. The licence might also include a co-operation component for research and development, regulating technology transfer and further development.

Licensing know-how additionally requires a high level of trust between the licensor and licensee, since the know-how may well constitute a trade secret of the licensor. Violation of the confidentiality provision in the licensing agreement could result in the know-how losing its status as a trade secret with potential consequences for the licensor's business. There are also various reasons to keep a patent application secret until it is mandatory to publish it, so confidentiality is also important in the preliminary phase.

Scope: exclusive or non-exclusive

Experience has shown that merely distinguishing between exclusive and non-exclusive licences is too simplistic a model. Whether or not a licence should be granted exclusively or non-exclusively depends on many factors, such as the sector, the technology concerned etc. For example, a licence as a part of a technical standard package in the telecommunications industry (where the entire patent package is licensed on pre-defined terms) is very different from a one-off licence for a specific patent. Nevertheless, the scope of the licence can be limited in many different ways so that even if a licence provides exclusivity, this may still result in a narrower scope than a broad non-exclusive licence. Several parameters can be combined in different ways to add up to the scope.

So, for example, if a licensor suggests 'a non-exclusive licence to use patent X worldwide', this might be problematic for different reasons. For one thing, it fails to define exactly what the licensee can do with the licence or which applications it covers. Compare this with 'an exclusive licence to patent X to manufacture Y products intended for pets in country Z'. Below are several key recommendations regarding the scope of licensing:

- Be specific about the scope of the licence. Consider all alternatives with an open mind: do not assume that a non-exclusive licence is necessarily best suited to your situation or the most attractive to the licensee. For example, a non-exclusive licence may not be attractive enough if the licensee needs to make further investments. Also, keep in mind that once you grant a non-exclusive licence, you limit your opportunities to grant an exclusive licence. Consider what the licensee needs for its own business case.

- An exclusive licence should ideally be tied to milestones of some sort, such as a certain number of products sold. If the milestones are not met within a certain time frame, then either the licence should be turned into a non-exclusive licence or the licensor should have the possibility of terminating it altogether. Another option is to define incremental minimum royalties to be paid.

- If exclusivity is granted, it is wise to consider competition law issues, in particular when the licence could result in a relatively large market share.

Unlocking multiple revenue streams

Technology owners have several options to develop business models that benefit from licensing opportunities. This is facilitated by the diversity of means to set up tailored contractual arrangements allowing them to create win-win relationships. However, specific challenges may arise, for example when innovative technologies have no ready-made market as they themselves create new business opportunities. An additional effort is required to achieve the intended commercial impact while the technology itself is being further developed and refined. This applies in particular to platforms or enabling technologies with multiple applications.

To give a concrete example, a company called WoodWelding[13] had invented a method for using ultrasonic waves to infuse thermoplastics into wood and other porous materials. The technology created a near-instant, very stable bond that could be used to attach hardware or fuse pieces of an assembly without using adhesives or fasteners. So while the inventors had come up with an intriguing technology, they had trouble positioning it in the market due to the numerous potential fields of use.

The typical advice in such a situation is to find the killer application in an industry with low-entry barriers, focus on that application and then re-invest the earnings to explore other options. In line with that, the most market-ready applications have to be identified. In addition, in order to determine where the technology can be applied first you need to understand the market: what is its size and growth potential, who are your potential partners, is the market ready to take up new technologies, what is the potential for market penetration?

Oxeon followed exactly that route and combined selling its own products with licensing them for non-competing applications (model D). In contrast, WoodWelding focused on licensing (model C) and, for each selected field of use, decided to grant an exclusive licence to a single player in order to motivate that partner to invest in the co-development of market-ready solutions. This model requires a unique field of use to be defined for each licensee.

Since each improvement to the platform technology can potentially benefit licensees in multiple fields, it was decided to include a kind of cross- or back-licence. As a result, each co-development agreement had the potential to improve the situation for each licensee but also avoided potential future FTO challenges from new inventions down the value chain.

Because this licensing model provided multiple revenue streams early in the company's life, it supported bootstrapping. In other words, it enabled the licensor to finance further R&D efforts, IP portfolio management and the acquisition of new licensees with the revenues it generated rather than with third-party risk capital.

Many companies and technology transfer offices struggle with similar challenges. A licensing approach like the one applied by WoodWelding makes it possible to unlock untapped value. A prerequisite for such an approach is to establish and maintain a strong IP portfolio based on the initial invention and to add patents that protect follow-on inventions, different fields of use and related technical developments. A key business asset in such an approach, moreover, is broad geographical protection that covers all key markets and production sites.

• *Any opinions expressed in this article are those of the authors and not necessarily those of the European Patent Office.*

• *Tailored licensing agreements can be complex as many different, non-obvious options must be considered and compliance with national and international regulations is crucial. Therefore, experiences described in this article should not be interpreted as legal advice. We recommend involving specialized lawyers in the implementation of an intended licence transaction.*

• *The full version of this article first appeared under the title 'Licensing-based business models' in a special technology transfer edition of les Nouvelles, the Journal of the Licensing Executives Society, published in in partnership with the European IP Helpdesk and the European Patent Office in June 2022. More details at: www.epo.org/business-decision-makers.*

For details of the **High-growth technology business initiative**, see www.epo.org/high-technology-businesses. To stay updated, follow the High-growth technology business community on www.linkedin.com/company/ htbcommunity.

Bowman Heiden is co-director of the Centre for Intellectual Property at the University of Gothenburg, Chalmers University of Technology and the Norwegian University of Science and Technology.

Thomas Bereuter is innovation support programme area manager at the European Patent Academy of the European Patent Office in Munich.

Notes

1. https://www.upcounsel.com/cross-licensing-agreement (accessed 22/03/2022).
2. LESI, IP Valuation Business Briefing, May 2020, https://www.lesi.org/publications/business-briefings (accessed 22/03/2022).
3. Wim Vanhaverbeke, *Managing open innovation in SMEs*, Cambridge University Press, 2017, ISBN 9781139680981.
4. A combination of co-operator and competitor used to denote entities which usually engage as competitors but may also co-operate to achieve potential win-win situations.
5. See www.epo.org/technology-transfer-case-studies.
6. See www.epo.org/technology-transfer-case-studies#cubicure and www.epo.org/technology-transfer-case-studies#blubrake.
7. See www.epo.org/sme-case-studies#webdyn.
8. See www.epo.org/technology-transfer-case-studies#dermis.
9. See www.epo.org/sme-case-studies#fractus.
10. See www.epo.org/sme-case-studies#marinomed.
11. See www.epo.org/technology-transfer-case-studies#oxeon.
12. See www.epo.org/technology-transfer-case-studies#fos4x.
13. Gerhard Plasonig, Pernilla Kvist, Martina Serafini & Evan LaBuzetta, 'Collaborating For Growth: The Novel Cross-Licensing Model That Wood Welding SA Used To Break Into New Markets Globally', *les Nouvelles,* 107-110 (2015), June issue.

6.

IP OPTIONS AFTER THE
UNITARY PATENT AND BREXIT

Opt in? Opt out? Oppose? Ilya Kazi at IK-IP weighs up the outlook for cost-effective European strategies for patents, trade marks and designs

Shortly a unitary patent (UP) will finally come into effect covering the European Union. The UP potentially affects enforcement and costs for patents in Europe. Imminent decisions are needed for patent applications coming up to grant. Brexit has already affected EU designs and trade marks. So the selection of a simple cost-effective European IP strategy is far from intuitive.

Currently, the European Patent Office centrally grants patents which are then validated (and translated in some countries) after which they become separate national rights subject to national courts. Enforcement actions covering several countries, although rare, could duplicate costs for multiple sets of advisors. Instead, it will become possible to designate a UP that can be enforced or revoked centrally in a new system of courts. It will stand, fall and renew as a single asset.

When Germany takes a procedural step (now expected in early 2023), a sunrise period of three months will start before the Unified Patent Court (UPC) comes into full effect. The two systems will co-exist for some time. Significantly, oppositions will remain.

Confusingly, the EPO reach is broader than both the EU and the UPC. The EPO has 38 member states, including the United Kingdom. Trademarks and designs are handled by the EU Intellectual Property Office which is restricted precisely to the 27 EU states and which has seen practical changes since the UK left the EU. The UP is restricted to EU states but not all have signed up.

Opting in, opting out, what's it all about?

IP owners will be able to continue for some years with the existing validation in selected countries (and individual renewal, enforcement and revocation) or to opt for a UP. The UP will become the default, so you have to opt out, if you don't want its effects. If a central action is taken before you opt out, you can't opt out later. There has been suggestion of some urgency to decide. However, you will probably know if someone is likely to apply for central revocation and you should certainly know if you are going to apply to enforce a patent. It is likely you will be looking at oppositions first anyway. Nonetheless, it makes sense to get your plan in order. There are legalities and formalities to follow and costs to manage. Pre-sunrise, discounts may be available to register your opt-out.

Why opt in?

Many companies, small and large, opt to validate patents in only a few European countries, typically the UK, France and Germany, sometimes the Netherlands. If they can prevent sale in the larger markets and where the court systems are known, then it is unlikely to be worth competitors selling in only the smaller markets. So, in practice the existing system has served many companies tolerably. Pharmaceuticals and others with high-value sales across Europe are a notable exception.

It will however now be possible and cost effective to validate a patent in the entirety of Europe. If you have significant sales and competition in the smaller markets, both the ability to get protection and to enforce it EU wide could be a benefit.

Why opt out?

Patent offices generally subsidise initial grants with renewal fees paid later, which increase significantly as time passes (the logic being if you are paying annuities after 20 years, the patent is valuable to you). As annuities become more expensive and as the technology covered by the patent ages, it is possible to manage costs gracefully by dropping renewal in countries of less importance but still keeping alive core countries. UP renewal fees are expected to be pitched at a cost similar to three or four countries but there is no guarantee or precedent. It is possible that a decade hence, there will be an expensive binary choice to keep or maintain a patent for the whole EU.

The corollary to central enforcement is central revocation. Although it is hoped the new UP courts will be high quality, procedures, judges and precedents have not been tested. Courts and tribunals are always variable. On patent matters, history shows they do not always reach the same conclusions on similar facts. There is concern that all rights in Europe could be lost with all eggs in one basket following a bad decision.

Lower costs, useful protection

If your commercial profile is satisfied by having patents in key markets (and, for example, you are used to validating in the UK, France, Germany and maybe a couple of others), stick with the existing system. If you are just starting out and IP isn't the life blood of your company the same probably applies. Opt out, validate in the key countries only. If you validate a bit more widely, you can opt in later when you have seen how the courts develop and if you are happy having your renewals tied together.

IP more central, more budget

You should be actively considering your divisional application strategy as you come up to allowance. You might then consider selecting one case for a UP and another for a national validation strategy with different balances of validity and breadth. You might be filing national and European cases in parallel in some cases and/or utility models. Now is the time to reflect on how you will validate, renew, enforce and mitigate the threats for the 20-year lifetime of your existing IP.

Oppositions

Under the UP, EPO oppositions gain extra significance. Here's why. They can only be filed within nine months of grant and result in central revocation, similar to the UP. However, the difference is cost. The fees for an opposition are typically between €10,000 and €100,000, unless it's a complex case. A UP case is likely to be an order of magnitude higher, closer to litigation costs. The amount of litigation under the UP is likely to increase, that is after all what the system has been designed for. Previously, if a small competitor in another country suspected you were infringing a patent, they would have to question seriously the merits of launching an action. Now it will be much easier.

If you don't want to become embroiled in expensive litigation in a UP court, you should seriously consider adopting a pro-active approach to monitoring competitors' IP and putting steps in place to oppose where appropriate to head off threats. Unlike the UP, it can be anonymous. You can probably oppose and blunt a dozen or more patents for the price of litigating one. That does not even count the potentially large financial and reputational damage and inconvenience of being found to infringe if you lose.

UP jurisdictions

Brexit and patents

Whereas trade marks and designs were immediately impacted, the EPO continued unchanged and patents were not affected up until now. The UK and Germany have traditionally been major jurisdictions for enforcing and challenging patents in Europe. The UK was due to hold one of the courts expected to be the most active prior to Brexit but no more. However, the UK remains in the EPO and although outside the UP system is likely to remain one of the more important jurisdictions. The English courts have a good reputation for considered patent judgements. The UK is not alone in being outside the UPC jurisdiction.

UP and EPO members

The UP is open to the 27 EU member states but is not an EU institution. At present Spain, Croatia and Poland are all in the EU but have indicated that they do not intend to participate. Of the remaining 24, only 17 at the time of writing are ready to go ahead although more are expected to join. On 30 June 2022 Ireland announced its intention to hold a referendum on membership of the UP. Incidentally, it has upset the plans of many UK solicitors who were relying on Ireland being a member to gain rights of audience. The EPO extends to 38 member states so there will always be countries covered by an EPO grant that are not subject to the UP and it is likely that several EU states will hold out for at least some time to come.

Trade marks and designs

To recap, the UPC will not start to enforce EU trade mark or design rights, which will continue to be enforced strictly EU wide (ie, excluding the UK). It is relatively straightforward to obtain parallel UK and EU registrations and many UK firms offer discounted fixed fee packages for obtaining both together.

However, changes observed since Brexit (in part due to the end of examiner exchange with the UK Intellectual Property Office and an outflow of native English speakers) are an increase in unusual objections that marks are descriptive in the EU based on a bare similarity to English dictionary words. So we are seeing more different approaches and outcomes in the UK and EU for the same mark.

For new brands we do not recommend expending excess effort trying to predict borderline cases as there is simply insufficient consistency. It can often be worth trying to obtain a mark even if expecting resistance. Registrations are being gained in the UK and EU when an academic analysis might suggest it was likely to be problematic. Conversely some marks which have gone sailing through one office (rightly) have faced surprising objections in the other.

With designs on the other hand we are now sometimes seeing objections from the UK to an item being functional when the same design is registered without objection in the EU.

Summary

If you currently only validate European patents in a few countries or are an SME, then opting out and validating in the same countries is probably your simplest strategy.

If you haven't considered oppositions and a strategy for watching your competitors, then it is worth looking into now, as there is a greater likelihood of unwanted litigation in future.

For trade marks, take an early view on your prospects for developing a consistent brand in the UK and EU.

If you are a larger company or have hopes of growing into one, take a step back and explore what you want your IP portfolio to look like in five or ten years: what are the threats, how you can mitigate them and what ongoing costs you can expect? Now is the time to look ahead.

Ilya Kazi is a UK chartered patent attorney, a European patent attorney and a qualified English High Court litigator. Until Brexit, he was also a qualified EU trade mark and design attorney. He has handled approximately 5000 European patent applications, a hundred oppositions and a major UK High Court litigation. He was a senior partner in a firm he grew to over 200 people. In 2020, he founded IK-IP to offer more commercially focused, predictably priced advice on all EU IP matters. The practice is growing rapidly.

Ilya has been repeatedly named as a leading global IP strategist by major publications. Despite often being deeply involved in IP cases, he believes in engaging personally with new clients, whether large or small, to make sure they receive the right level of strategic input all along the way without being deterred by the cost of obtaining it. Further details at: www.ik-ip.com.

7.
FREEDOM TO GROW

Like chess, make the right moves at the right moment to clear your path to market, says Nicola Baker-Munton at Stratagem

It is often helpful to think of an intellectual property strategy in terms of chess moves. The first move you make, such as a pawn going one square forward, can seem like a simple move, but its influence on the rest of what may be a complex game can be critical. Early planning of an IP strategy is key to a good outcome whether the aim is an investment, trade sale or listing on the stock market. Although the result may seem a long way off, just as the pieces need to be in the right place on the board at the right time for successful moves in chess, so too do key decisions need to be made early on for there to be successful strategy outcomes in business.

Freedom to market

Freedom to market is vital to determining the eventual outcome of your venture. That means freedom from the threat of infringement of a third party's IP rights. Most people think solely of freedom to operate

(FTO) under third-party patents, but you should not ignore the freedom to operate under contract, ie, binding terms that prevent you from using something commercially. Use of a third party's confidential know-how or material has a tendency to become public eventually and so use of vectors, cell-lines, software or images can all cause issues of freedom to operate. How deeply embedded they are in what you are offering will determine the extent to which someone sues you. Just as the knight in chess can move in an L-shape and leapfrog other pieces, springboarding off the use of a third party's confidential materials, even if the final product is one leap away from the original use, it can still become an issue if later publications are made or information is needed to support a patent filing or a drug application for example.

Landscape the technology

So why do we need to clear the path to market ahead of arriving there? For a start the investment in research and development is substantial. So before you invest any significant sums, but only once you have clarity on the product details or the process or service elements, you should really undertake an FTO search and analysis of potentially relevant published patents and applications.

Prior to a full FTO search and analysis, ie, before the product or process is well defined, you can landscape the area, and there are products out there that will give you useful statistics about how many companies are working in your field, even giving you the names and numbers of patents filed. It will give you a feel for how busy the sector is, although is not representative of what is needed to establish freedom from the threat of a patent infringement suit that could be launched against you.

Investor expectations

There are good internal reasons to undertake an FTO search and analysis, notably to protect your own investment and make sure your money is not being wasted. But there is an external reason too. If you plan to partner with a larger company for further development, they will want to know if you have established FTO. In industry, any project in which at least some FTO work has been undertaken rises up the pile, so it does provide a competitive advantage. Although early planning won't stop a potential partner from verifying this or even carrying out a full assessment of their own, it will hopefully mean that you have already identified any showstoppers. Investors or trade acquirers will similarly want to know that there is a clear path to market and are likely to ask for representations or warranties. At Stratagem, we once helped a company list on the AIM market with a known potential FTO issue, but as we had identified it, evaluated the risk and built its mitigation into the plan, it was accepted by the market.

Impact on valuation

Another reason for undertaking an FTO search and analysis is that it can have a positive effect on your company's valuation. In the past, we have seen some astonishingly expensive and in-depth FTO analyses undertaken by investors who have not then invested. In some cases because they did not like the management team, but in most because they, or more importantly their patent lawyers, dug an enormous hole, convincing themselves that there was an issue, when there was not.

By conducting FTO searches or analyses, issues can be identified. Potential investors or partners are then less likely to find something. If they do, however relevant, it is less likely to cause battles to rage over the impact on valuation. As such, undertaking FTO work early on, allows you to get the other side's lawyers to see reason, which makes life much easier.

Your search

When undertaking a search to identify potentially relevant patents, it should cover keywords and classification codes used by patent offices, as well as company and individual names. It should also cover the product, the processes by which it is made, any formulations, devices by which it is delivered etc. The best results come when a company works with IP professionals to establish the right search protocol and find as much relevant literature as is available from the outset.

Often, FTO can be seen as a game, but testing searchers by not revealing what you already know is counterproductive. Collaboration helps when different patent applicants describe something using synonyms and variations in terminology. Some of the hardest subjects to search are computer-implemented inventions, which is rarely how they are described. They are generally referred to as a process, an algorithm or the technical effect they are trying to achieve. Searching in this way is similar to the queen in chess. As she can move in any direction for any number of squares, she provides comprehensive cover of the whole board, just as the FTO analysis should aim to do, although her next move can be hard to predict.

Your analysis

Your next step is analysis of the search. Any patent found that might pose a problem needs further investigation. For instance, whether it is still in force (ie, fees have to be paid every year, or every 3½ years in the United States); if it is still alive now or will be by the time you plan to launch, it needs review. In the meantime, you could claim a research exemption or carry out the development work in a non-patented territory. Checking the term of a patent (when it will expire) is reasonably straightforward in most territories, as it is 20 years from filing or 21 years from the first priority filing (with up to five years extension for specific medical products). In the US however, you need to look out for PTA (Patent Term Adjustment, awarded for delays in the Patent Office); the longest of which we have seen is six years. When carrying out an analysis of the search, look out for terminal disclaimers in the US, as these have the opposite effect. If the patent is one of a family, its term may be reduced so it is no longer than one of its earlier family members.

Patent interpretation

Assuming you have not already discounted the patent, it now requires deeper review. The key is to look at, but not focus entirely on, the claims of the patent. If a patent is granted, then the claims are fixed, which become the focus of your analysis. If a patent application is still pending it is possible for the claims to change significantly. It is usual, but not certain, that claims tend to narrow rather than broaden.

Sometimes a review of what is called the file wrapper (the exchanges between an applicant and an examiner) can provide an effective guide to how the claims are faring, but, until the point of grant, the king is still in play. The claims are usually what an applicant hopes to obtain and so often give the broadest aspect, but not always. Other inventions can lurk in the specification and can be pulled out into a 'sister' divisional or continuation application, as long as there is a patent still pending. So it is key to review the whole document and not just the claims, unless everything in the family is granted and then focusing on the claims is acceptable.

When companies try to review patents for themselves, often the opposite is the problem. They tend to read the whole patent and discount it on the basis of the owner doing something different. However, if the disclosure supports a claim that is broad enough to cover what the client is doing, the fact that the examples or process described are different, does not get them off the hook.

The interpretation of claims is a real art. It not only requires a specialist to review them, but often a local specialist, as claims are interpreted differently in different jurisdictions. If there are clear elements required by the claims that are not in your product, you will not infringe. Be careful to look at all the so-called 'independent claims', as these are the ones that do not refer back to other claims. They stand alone. Within one granted patent, they can be of different scopes. The most relevant could be claim 136 (true story).

Winning combinations

To win the chess game, you not only have to consider the moves you want to make, but also predict the other side's strategy. The other side might be investors or trade partners who need to know that their investment will be sound, so they can be provided with a return on their investment; or they might be a competitor.

When you undertake searches or analyses and you find a problem, you still have options: all is not lost. Of course, you can consider stopping what you are doing or find a workaround, if you are confident that the scope of the claims will not change. It is quite often possible to acquire the patent, as we have done many times, so turning a threat into an opportunity. Almost as good is to exclusively license the patent, as long as you have all the rights of enforcement written into the licence. If that is not possible, a simple non-exclusive licence will give you freedom from the threat of infringement to progress your product or process to market.

FTO is not static. Your products and processes change and so does the patent pool. You have a multitude of different options available and your competitors' options are shifting too, so watch their filings and carry out fresh searches to ensure nothing new emerges. Even pieces that don't move directly can become important, if used strategically with the pieces placed around them.

Nicola Baker-Munton is the founder and executive chair of Stratagem IPM. She is a UK and European patent attorney with a joint honours degree in biology and biochemistry. During her nine years as an industrial practitioner at the Wellcome Foundation and four years in the private sector, Nicola recognised the requirement for more assistance with managing IP earlier in the development of technologies and with commercialization throughout the technology/product lifecycle. Nicola founded Stratagem IPM in 1999. With steady growth it has become a leading specialist in providing proactive strategic management of IP portfolios from inception through development to market, and from academia through start-up to stock market listing. Further details: www.strategemipm.co.uk.

8.
LEAN IP MANAGEMENT

Don't stockpile your intellectual property, says Oliver Baldus at Splanemann. Instead, replace the internal view of protecting ideas with an external view of creating value to make yourself up to 90 percent more efficient

Lean IP management allows optimum use of scarce company resources to support and improve general business goals. Lean IP management interprets IP in a much broader way than only protecting individual inventions. Instead, lean IP gives an integrated and cross-linked approach to general operations of the firm, opening up the potential to reduce the cost of IP by up to 90 percent or make similar improvements in the impact it makes.

Today's IP world

Today's patent portfolios are often based on an internal view of the firm that relies on the notion that self-generated ideas always require optimum IP protection. This assumption is made regardless of whether there will be a later infringer to the protected idea in the future or not. Thus, currently many firms hold large numbers of patents resulting from their own research activities for which they never would be willing to pay if they were purchased from a third party.

In this context winning with IP sounds like a brilliant idea. However, the question remains what is exactly meant with the term winning in complex IP situations. In principle, it could describe numerous outcomes, like defeating an opponent, living in peaceful co-existence or being invulnerable. In terms of IP, winning is often left unspecified.

The lack of commitment to distinct business goals supported by IP additionally leads to costly, unspecified and unco-ordinated strategies under the sentimental premise: the more, the better. Undifferentiated brute force IP strategies, however, automatically create huge portfolios of diverging IP rights and waste valuable company resources. Therefore, many current portfolios can be best described as huge piles of possible weapons containing many useless toy rifles among a few dangerous atomic missiles.

The fog of IP

Since the IP world is complex, it automatically involves significant uncertainties. In the realm of war, the former Prussian general and military theorist Carl von Clausewitz described such a situation as:

> War is the realm of uncertainty; three-quarters of the factors on which action in war is based are wrapped in a fog of greater or lesser uncertainty. A sensitive and discriminating judgment is called for; a skilled intelligence to scent out the truth.

Even in the IP world this profound judgement of the old general is nowadays truer than ever and can be directly translated as 'fog of IP'. Also, in the realm of IP it is generally not possible to ever predict future IP situations. For example, it is unforeseeable if an infringement occurs based on a yet non-granted patent application, a new patent destroying prior art is surprisingly found, or a competitor launches a successful opposition. These are only three prominent examples of uncertainty among thousands that exist in the IP world. Having this in mind, we should ask today whether we can get rid of the ancient approach of simply relying on more weapons, but to develop better, modern and sophisticated IP strategies that make smarter use of existing conditions? As the quotation already suggests, these new IP strategies take their cue from von Clausewitz's skilled intelligence.

The principle of lean

Lean strategies give you this sensitive and discriminating judgement. Lean production and management have been widely accepted for decades, based on the principle that scarce financial and human resources should be deployed as efficiently as possible. Lean strategies get the most out of available resources and yield the highest outcomes.

Consequently, all resources should be deployed so the greatest gains are achieved. Likewise, these lean concepts imply that all non-value-adding activities within a system must be eliminated. In an evolutionary business world, these lean principles can put companies at a significant advantage compared to their competitors.

Lean IP management

As in all conventional lean strategies, these principles are also core elements of lean IP management. Lean IP management focuses on eliminating non-value-adding IP rights and leveraging the remaining value-adding IP rights only where they stand to have the most impact.

Eliminating non-value-adding IP activities

The sole criterion for distinguishing value-adding IP from non-value adding is the market potential of the protected subject matter. The value of a patent must be directly derived from the market value of the protected innovation. Thus, in lean IP, all rights for products that are not economically interesting are abandoned. It makes no sense to hold costly prohibition rights for products that no one wants to use anyway. In such cases, prohibition rights are existent but cannot be exerted due to the lack of an infringer: in terms of warfare, they represent toy rifles that can't hit any target.

Lean IP management replaces the former internal view of protecting company ideas by an external view that sees IP rights from a market perspective. Only those IP rights for which a potential buyer would be willing to pay are maintained. Under this criterion, costly non-value-adding IP is cut, leaving an arsenal of powerful IP assets whose principal impact to a third party is guaranteed.

More impact for IP assets

However, once established, the question remains how to best use this refined arsenal in the surrounding business world. Options range from deterrence to attack.

Attack actively uses IP rights as weapons to generate desired outcomes, such as gaining licence fees from a competitor. In contrast, deterrence serves as a wall of defence against any hostility. However, not every IP arsenal is suited to any option and any target. IP has the specific characteristic that it has no general impact, but can only be used for particular targets, ie, possible infringers.

Consequently, lean IP primarily identifies winning business strategies that could be additionally supported by own IP rights. These business strategies depend on more than directly earning licence fees. They could include gaining market shares, lowering procurement costs, preparing company acquisitions or supporting general negotiations.

In all these situations IP rights can be used as an effective bargaining chip to exert pressure on the involved party. In fact, the traditional focus on licence fees is only one business strategy among thousands in lean IP management.

Once business goals are defined, a suitable IP target can be identified, whether it's a competitor, a supplier or a user. It then becomes possible to make a distinction between supporting and non-supporting IP assets within a strategy. After first removing non-value-adding IP, the next step of lean IP consists in sorting out non-supporting IP rights.

In this context, lean patent applications add extra value to the company. In contrast to regular patent applications, they directly envisage and claim subject matter which has sufficient market potential and which supports the identified business strategies. Ideally, they are written with the intention of hitting a chosen target. In contrast to the many non-directional, verbose patent applications we currently see, they are easier to prepare, more focused and much easier to prosecute. Since they are exclusively related to protecting subject matter that has market potential, they are automatically value-adding assets.

Establishing IP superiority

Attack options, like actively using IP rights as a bargaining chip or a lever in negotiations, must always be based on IP superiority. Within the crystalized business strategy, a successful attack is only reasonable if the IP impact on the target is larger than the target's IP impact on you. So, if you are vulnerable to retaliation, it excludes this option.

To this end, lean IP analyzes possible countermeasures by the target. Only if adverse IP retaliation can be excluded, can your IP rights be effectively used to foster and enforce self-defined business goals.

Therefore, your IP position must be evaluated and, if necessary, expanded until superiority with respect to your target is reached. It could be achieved by a concerted filing of lean patent applications that directly fall within the scope of the target of your strategy. In addition, adverse IP, like hostile patent applications on your technology, are monitored and evaluated. These possible hostile rights are deliberately cut and disabled by your own activities, like filing oppositions or starting nullity proceedings.

Once a sufficient IP superiority is reached, there are no remaining obstacles to using IP rights in successfully supporting business strategies that involve a third party. IP superiority creates a credible threat to encourage the target's amenability. In this case, business strategies, such as reducing procurement costs, cutting a competitor's market share or raising sales prices can be realized. IP superiority overcomes a target's resistance and brings it into line with your business goals.

Conclusion

Lean IP is a matter of choice in complex situations and allows a sensitive and discriminating judgement about what value IP adds or supports. It is the perfect tool for navigating the uncertainty associated with the fog of IP. It is directed to an intelligent and combined use of measures that each enhances the others.

Lean IP management represents the most efficient tool for employing IP rights and integrating them into broader business challenges. When seen not only from an IP perspective of protecting inventions but also from a higher business level, strategic goals can be more reliably reached and the efficiency of IP budgets can improve by up to 90 percent. This is how we define winning with IP.

Dr Oliver Baldus is a German as well as a European patent attorney and a partner at Splanemann LLP in Munich, which is one of the oldest law firms in Germany. He holds degrees in physics, economics, and European intellectual property law. He is the author of numerous articles on economic aspects of patents and lean IP management. In addition, he wrote the recent benchmark book on claim interpretation and wording, as well as various articles on protecting artificial intelligence and software applications.

9.
HOW INTELLECTUAL ASSETS
IMPACT EXIT VALUE

The value that a business achieves at exit is heavily influenced by three intellectual assets, says Juergen Graner at the High-growth Technology Business Initiative: its technology, its brand and its operational excellence

Owners of high-growth technology businesses should decide at an early stage whether they are developing their company for continuation as an independent organization (build to grow) or for an exit (build to sell). They are two fundamentally different strategies open to the business leader when building a company.

The ultimate goal when employing a build-to-grow strategy is to continue the business in perpetuity. On the other hand, a build-to-sell strategy has the clear goal of selling the business at a certain point in the future.

Key strategic decisions are made with this goal in mind and differ if the time horizon is one to three years, three to five years, or five to ten years. Anything significantly below a twelve-month time horizon tends to be a patch-to-sell approach with limited options for creating value.

A build-to-grow strategy is generally associated with a family or lifestyle business. It also applies to IPOs (initial public offerings). A build-to-sell strategy is often driven by risk reduction needs and cash-out desires of the business owners. Moreover, investor needs are an important factor to build a business with a clear exit horizon in mind. In high-growth technology businesses, the capital requirements are often so significant that bootstrapping (building a company without external equity financing) is not an option. Moreover, since debt funding is limited by the collateral that a business owner can put up, most high-growth businesses require equity funding. The majority of equity financing comes from funds with a limited lifetime (usually ten years). Therefore, they need to cash in on their investment to realize a positive return on investment at some point. This means that equity funding generally comes with the requirement for a build-to-sell strategy and a time frame dictated by the remaining life of the fund providing the money.

The three intellectual assets (IAs), technology, brand, and operational excellence, are generally dominant value drivers for an exit deal. Developing a sound portfolio of IAs over many years before the exit will not only provide the business owners with an increased exit valuation, it will also give the company a sustainable competitive advantage in the event a planned exit does not take place or is delayed.

Since IAs cannot be established at short notice, the process of building a sound IA portfolio must begin many years beforehand. Ideally, a dedicated board function will have prime responsibility for the sellability of the business, allowing the chief executive to remain focused on managing day-to-day operations with a steady eye on the customers. Continuous management of the exit process years in advance and for some time after the exit transaction is crucial to the best possible outcome.

Three pricing elements

The purchase price, the first element, is the overall price that the buyer is willing to pay to acquire a business. In the case of an equity deal, the buyer receives full ownership in the seller's company (provided they buy a hundred percent of the business, although in some cases the buyer might only acquire a certain percentage). In the event of an asset deal, the buyer purchases only specific assets of the business.

As a rule, however, the purchase price is not the amount that the seller will receive once the deal is closed. In most cases, the buyer will require the seller to provide binding promises (contractually fixed under representations, warranties and indemnifications) that certain assumptions about the business are correct. One simple example is that the inventory actually represents the value claimed by the seller. To secure these promises, the buyer will ask that a certain portion of the purchase price (depending on the industry and the risks perceived by the buyer) be deposited in an escrow account as a holdback, managed by an escrow agent. This escrow holdback, the second pricing element, is subsequently released either to the seller or to the buyer, based on contractually defined terms and timelines. The initial price paid is thus the adjusted purchase price, calculated as the agreed purchase price minus the escrow holdback, ownership of which is only determined throughout the escrow period.

Companies that have been set up for high performance under new ownership through a solid build-to-sell process and supported by a strong IA portfolio have the potential to benefit from an additional earn-out, the third pricing element. An earn-out provides supplementary payments over and above the agreed purchase price for achieving defined performance criteria. In most cases, these performance criteria are based on sales performance. However, along with countless other options, they could also include certain milestones in a product development process.

While the escrow holdback has the potential to reduce the agreed purchase price, the earn-out can add to it. The tricky part about receiving earn-outs is that, by this point, control over the performance has shifted to the new owner and any success depends not only on the right preparation on the part of the seller but also on the co-operation of the buyer. While certain requirements may be put in place by the seller to enable earn-out performance, the main driver here is business logic combined with management support from the seller's team.

The following example from the life science industry illustrates the possible impact of escrow holdback and earn-out on the actual amount received by the seller (parameters depend on individual situations and industries). With a purchase price of $50 million, plus a 20 percent escrow holdback and a $20 million earn-out, the difference between a worst-case scenario (all the escrow holdback is kept by the buyer and no earn-out is paid = $40 million exit deal value) and a best-case scenario (the entire escrow holdback is released to the seller and the full earn-out is achieved = $70 million) would be $30 million. This translates to a 75 percent higher overall exit price if the business was well prepared in a build-to-sell process and the implementation phase went according to plan. IAs are major contributors and increase the likelihood of a higher purchase price in the first place and a higher overall exit deal.

General assets

General assets typically include customers (expressed in revenue), cost structure (expressed in gross margin and profitability), established contracts, equipment, inventory, work in progress and team members. As the foundation of any business valuation, they have a substantial impact on the purchase price because they are relatively easy for the acquirer to evaluate in a due diligence process.

Since an escrow agreement needs clear trigger points to determine whether the seller or the buyer receives the retained funds, general assets also have a huge impact on the escrow holdback.

While general assets may serve as the foundation of an earn-out (eg, equipment with significant spare capacity enables the sales team to sell more products), their impact on it is usually low.

Technology assets

Strong technology IAs combine the technology intellectual property, mainly secured by patents and trade secrets, with the know-how of the team. For a company with a strong technology portfolio, the impact of technology on the purchase price can be significant, especially when it gives the business a sustainable competitive advantage. For example, patent-protected technology with a clear enforcement and freedom-to-operate position that allows the company to exclude competitors for a relevant period of time increases value as the current performance and growth pattern is more likely to continue.

The impact of technology on the escrow holdback tends to be low, as it is relatively difficult to find trigger points that would provide an escrow release payment to one of the parties. One example in which technology might have an impact on the escrow holdback is a pending patent lawsuit that could threaten a business's technology foundation where winning or losing patent litigation could determine the payout of an earmarked holdback.

From an earn-out perspective, technology can have a high impact on an agreed earn-out. This is especially true if, for example, the company owns platform technology that has only been tried and tested in one market segment but could be used to access one or several other markets. It could be part of an earn-out payment based on future sales in those new markets, provided the buyer agrees to enter those markets shortly after the deal is completed.

Brand assets

Strong brand IAs combine the brand's IP secured by trade marks with the ownership of customer mindshare, where individuals associate the brand with certain attributes.

A strong brand almost always has a powerful impact on the purchase price although the value is generally higher in business-to-consumer than in business-to-business focused companies. This is interesting as, in most cases, the seller's brand will be replaced with the buyer's brand. However, having a strong brand, where the task is not finding new customers who have positive associations with it, but transferring existing positive associations to a new brand in a controlled step-by-step process, is still of great value to a buyer.

Since a brand is generally easy to assess in a due diligence process, the impact of the brand on the escrow holdback is almost always low. One situation in which an escrow holdback might be impacted by the brand is when the acquired company does not own a registered trade mark with an uncontested status and there is reason to believe that the brand might actually violate existing trade mark rights of another company.

Earn-outs are usually based on future sales performance. Since great sales performance builds on a strong brand that has been established over many years, the impact of the brand on an earn-out is generally high. Moreover, the value increases if the buyer can use the seller's brand to expand the product portfolio quickly by targeting the seller's existing customers with its own products.

Operational excellence

Strong operational excellence IAs allow a company to consistently outperform others and combine the operational excellence IP secured by the operational systems with a culture that enables operational excellence.

Interestingly enough, operational excellence rarely has a direct impact on the purchase price from a valuation perspective. The reason is that it is difficult to prove the actual level of operational excellence in a company in a common due diligence process. Nevertheless, since operational excellence serves a company in a build-to-sell process during the development phase towards a sellable business and can ensure high sales growth, a high gross margin and fast product time-to-market, it has a significant intrinsic value affecting the purchase price.

Generally operational excellence does not have a major impact on the escrow holdback. Although some buyers might try to link the potential loss of key employees to an escrow trigger point, the truth is that this issue is better served with a special tie-in contract, retaining key employees for a certain period of time with defined bonus payments. Moreover, it would be very difficult to define escrow payment release trigger points for underperformance in terms of operational excellence.

Operational excellence really shines when it comes to the earn-out. A business developed for a sale through a solid build-to-sell process will have established at least a certain level of operational excellence that makes it easier to be integrated into the company structure of the buyer. Consequently, when the former chief executive steps down and a new one takes over, a business with operational excellence will continue to perform: this performance secures the earn-out payments. However, it is important that the seller still has someone in place to manage the transition carefully and ensure a smooth handover. This role is ideally performed by a person or a team that has been managing the build-to-sell process since the development phase and is therefore familiar with the company.

Conclusion

IAs are a significant contributor to an exit deal's value and need to be established over many years during the development phase of a business.

		Purchase price	Escrow holdback	Earn-out
General assets		High	High	Low
Intellectual assets	Technology	High	Low	High
	Brand	High	Low	High
	Operational excellence	Low	Low	High

Figure 1: Impact of assets on the pricing elements of an exit deal

The secret to the success of an optimized exit is understanding that different assets have a different impact on the three pricing elements of an exit deal: purchase price, escrow holdback, and earn-out (see Figure 1). General assets have the highest impact on the adjusted purchase price (the purchase price minus the escrow holdback deposited in an escrow account) and little impact on an earn-out. Technology and brand IAs generally have a high impact on the purchase price and limited impact on the escrow holdback but are the key drivers for an earn-out. Operational excellence is an inconsequential outlier in the IA class as its impact on the purchase price is more intrinsic. On the other hand, it is usually the most important driver for earn-outs.

Therefore, an owner of a high-growth technology business should ensure that a proactive build-to-sell process is initiated at an early stage, developing a solid portfolio of IAs to secure the value of the business. In the event an exit does not materialize for any reason, these IAs will continue to be the backbone of the sustainable competitive advantage that the company has built. In any case, a business cannot go wrong with a strong IA portfolio.

Furthermore, if a business owner opts for a build-to-sell strategy, they should establish a build-to-sell function at board level in their company that is tasked with guiding the company from the development phase through the transaction phase and into the implementation phase. The business owner should focus on managing day-to-day operations with a steady eye on the customers, while the build-to-sell function's prime focus is the company's sellability.

• *The full version of this article first appeared in the June 2022 edition of les Nouvelles, the journal of the Licensing Executives Society under the title 'Build to sell powered by intellectual assets: a high-growth technology*

business perspective' and is available at: https://www.epo.org/learning/
materials/sme/high-growth-technology-businesses/decision-makers.
html.

Juergen Graner is founder and chief executive of Globalator in the United States, United Kingdom and Austria. He has experience as a chief executive in six countries on three continents and, over the course of his career, has coached over a hundred chief executives in creating value with strategic transactions. Juergen also regularly speaks at conferences and teaches on the subject of Transaction Based Growth Management™. He is a member of the HTB Task Force at EPO and the HGE Task Force at LESI.

10.
INNOVATING WITH
EDGE TECHNOLOGIES

As we stand between two technology eras, you can rely on being a genius, you can innovate as standard or, more profitably and predictably, you can change your mindset and process, says Robert Klinski at Patentship

Significant value is within reach for the numerous activities that are now being disrupted by edge technologies. Rules for how to practise disciplines such as accounting, legal, education and many others are being re-written.

At present, it is only a few who are fully realising this potential for innovation and intellectual property. Most find themselves missing out or falling short. Such outcomes are by no means inevitable. It is just a matter of how you go about it.

In this age of digital transformation, the prospect of a highly productive three-step strategy is opening up for those who can join up the pieces of disruptive ideas:

- Clearly articulate the challenge for your market.

- Set a technical problem for your engineers.

- Create a series of solutions that you can patent.

As a side effect, such an approach can radically improve the efficiency of patent portfolios in three significant respects:

- The chances of patenting an edge technology can significantly improve, reaching close to 90 percent in our experience.

- A switch from patents centred on technology to those inspired by the market will bring into focus the few that really make a return, giving more time to shed those that don't.

- Capital risks can also be reduced by investing proportionately more in IP, and less in research and development.

A disruptive mindset

You cannot adopt a conventional mindset in how you respond to edge technologies. You will be too far behind the curve in creating value from them.

Instead, take a disruptive cue from a pioneer such as Elon Musk at Tesla or from a breakthrough technology like blockchain. In both cases, the originality lies in articulating a problem that manifests itself in the market.

First, you have to grasp the size and shape of a non-technical challenge, such as autonomous mobility or a digital currency. Only then, do you pass it on to your engineering and IP teams to design a technical solution.

They may well feel uncomfortable about being asked to step outside the safe confines of their own domain. They may well tell you that you will struggle to tie down the IP.

However, if you can pair a disruptive insight with a technical solution, streaming them alongside each other, you have every chance of lining up IP that gives you an edge in accounting tech, legal tech or any other kind of tech.

Find the purpose, not the difference

Engineering teams are incremental by nature. They work on the basis of identifying improvements to existing technologies. They are typically responding to requests by their managers for more speed, less weight, more stability or better security.

Patent offices work in the same way. They look for the differences between your invention and the prior art. Like engineers, they are not responding to the market. They want a defined platform from which to start.

A breakthrough like blockchain doesn't even try to improve the prior art. It starts with a question such as how could we go about creating a secure digital currency? The solution, which links a chain of digital signatures across blocks of data, bypasses any directly comparable technologies. As an innovation, it manages to articulate what the market requires and frames the technical challenge in a way around which developers can invent.

Inventing on demand

Essentially, we are at a bottleneck between our old system of engineering and prior art, which relies on a spirit of incremental improvement, and a new system of disruptive insights and data innovation, based on edge technologies, such as artificial intelligence and blockchain.

The challenge is to build a bridge between the two. Don't feel that you have to be a genius like Elon Musk. Invention on demand is a process that you can follow. First, find the courage to think disruptively. Then deploy the strengths of your existing engineering and IP systems to create a technical solution and secure a commercial advantage.

It matters how you manage this sequence. If you think conventionally too soon, your chances of gaining a patent with edge technologies are probably 50 percent at best. If instead, you learn to invent on demand, our experience suggests that your odds rise to 90 percent.

In some cases, the gap between outcomes is much wider. From the point of view of a technology like 5G, engineering teams may see little scope for invention and no potential for patents. When configured from the perspective of the market, however, a rich stream of innovation opens up, which would otherwise have been missed.

As a technology, it builds on previous transmissions and protocols. The fundamental difference lies in how you can design the network. By using slices, you can scale it up or down, depending on whether you are making a phone call, screening augmented reality or sending signals to a driverless car. The speed and quality of the service are what matter in each case.

Designs for these 'network slices' are becoming a highly sought and lucrative form of IP. By adjusting its mindset and framing questions differently, a 5G operator can halts its slide towards commodity status and turn itself into a digital innovator.

Map the non-technical onto the technical

At first sight, many of your digital inventions will appear to lie beyond the scope of patents, the most reliable way of making a return on investments in technology. Historically, mental acts, including data, are excluded.

However, software inventions can be translated into the technical domains that patents require. Like a chameleon, it is a question of changing colour to match the demands of your environment, so making it possible for inventive algorithms with technical effect to gain protection.

On a digital gambling game, for instance, the patterns for displaying apples and oranges might have been inventive, but could not be patented. The resolution was to protect the underlying scheme for random signal processing without making any reference to the game.

In the same way, you can transfer inventions in accounting or educational software into a technical resolution that falls within the scope of a patent.

Technology management

The logic of such invention on demand depends on catching a technology at the right point, not too early, not too late, but just at the sweet spot when it stops emerging and starts to grow.

All technologies follow a lifecycle as they emerge, grow and mature. At the start, everything is new. There is no history. Comparisons are hard to draw. Platform IP can be secured at relatively little cost, even if it is hard to know which technology trend to follow and the risk-to-reward ratio is speculatively high.

At the growth stage, innovation becomes more incremental, driven more by R&D and less by inventors. Many more patents are filed, the scope for protection narrows, IP costs rise and the risk-to-reward ratios drop.

Once a technology matures, innovation plateaus, IP becomes expensive to maintain and the risk-to-reward ratio reaches its low point. Much of the budget is spent on enforcing the IP.

The focus of far too many companies is still on conservatively managing the risks in innovation and taking a view that is too centred on technology. The whole process is geared towards maintaining the status quo. By playing it safe, they end up with late-stage technologies that no one wants to buy.

IP portfolios

In conventional portfolios, only 1 to 3 percent of IP ends up having any significant value. The remainder is a legacy of the days when IP was considered a defensive necessity, rather than an active asset. Edge technologies present a second chance to run portfolios more efficiently.

Decisions about the value of an innovation can be made at the beginning, not after a technology has been created. More responsibility for them falls on business units and less on IP departments.

When the emphasis is on creating value in the market in this way, decisions about whether to invest in IP, as opposed to R&D, come more into focus. By buying in IP, instead of creating their own, companies can significantly reduce their capital risk and create an asset that it is similar in nature to a financial option or derivative. Here they are following the smart money.

IP investments

For those investors looking for exposure to high-growth technologies, the logic of patented inventions on demand is starting to make itself clear. Conventionally, early-stage investors pick a promising start-up and line up €10 million in equity. As a formula, it remains fraught with difficulty. Even the smartest investors only expect to make a significant return on one investment in ten.

The question many are asking themselves is: can we save ourselves the risk of losing all our capital, while still retaining the option for a gain on the upside? In other words, instead of investing in a 'hard asset', such as equity, can we use a 'soft asset' with the characteristics of a derivative?

In the case of technology, patents can be a highly effective equivalent. Under the Patent Co-operation Treaty, you can gain up to 31 months to determine whether to go ahead or not. The capital at risk is roughly 1 percent of the commitment to a start-up.

As a technique, it remains for now the domain of specialist investors, able to find the sweet spot at the point that an emerging technology establishes itself. However, the signs are clear that money is gravitating towards inventing on demand as a process and that the winners from digital transformation will be those who can best configure their innovations round insights into emerging sources of value.

Robert Klinski is a pioneering IP thinker and practitioner who is pursuing invention on demand in edge technologies. He started his career in radio signals at Siemens and Fraunhofer, before founding his own IP practice, Patentship, where he takes pride in acting for those with a mindset to grow disruptive technologies. His clients include Fortune 500 companies, start-ups and research institutions, as well as investors who believe patents offer a better return than start-ups.

11.
INVENTING WITH AI

Artificial intelligence is permeating all fields of invention and is now starting to make its own. Philipp Kühn and Martin Jacob at Uexküll & Stolberg consider the implication for intellectual property

Artificial intelligence is becoming increasingly important as a driver of significant technological and economic developments. AI has long since permeated our everyday lives in a wide variety of characteristics such as the digital voice assistants found on our smartphones, the chatbots that we struggle to distinguish from humans, medical image analysis and autonomous vehicles. Since AI can combine and analyze huge amounts of data faster than any human in a very short time, its use in combination with big data, cloud computing or the internet of things (IoT) offers companies the opportunity to optimize the speed of their solutions and services in a targeted manner. Taking into account that almost any technology can be equipped with AI, it can be expected that with the exponential progress of AI technology, the world around us, from leisure to business to health, will change exponentially.

The patent system is also facing new challenges, as patent offices have been seeing an exponential increase in AI-related patent applications for some time, according to recent reports from the World Intellectual Property Organization and the UK Intellectual Property Office. However, as AI continues to develop and become more widely used, companies are faced with the question of how to handle it when AI is significantly involved in an invention or makes one itself.

AI and the Fourth Industrial Revolution

AI, according to a definition by the European Patent Office, refers to the ability of computers and machines to perform intellectual tasks normally associated with humans, for example learning, reasoning or devising solutions to problems. AI often involves an iterative training process (machine learning), whereby an AI system is enabled to adapt to a specific problem before making appropriate decisions or suggesting independent interpretations.

The first approaches to the development of an AI already existed in the mid-1950s, when researchers discussed describing all aspects of learning and intelligence in such a way that a machine could be built to simulate these processes. A first approach to this was the chatbot, Eliza, in the 1960s, which was able to enter into dialogue with humans, but was not able to learn and was pre-programmed according to a certain logic.

Subsequent development focused primarily on providing expert systems that accumulate knowledge and support people in complex problems. A program developed by the University of Stanford, MYCIN, for example, was able to identify pathogens of infectious diseases on the basis of parameters and provide recommendations for suitable antibiotics.

Another milestone was Deep Blue, the chess computer from IBM, which in 1996 beat Gary Kasparov, who was the reigning world chess champion at that time. However, Deep Blue did not learn to play chess, but beat the world chess champion through pure computing power. Since then, AI development has made tremendous progress, due in part to the integration of efficient systems such as machine learning, deep learning and neural networks, as well as the availability of big data, large computing capacities and advanced algorithms. In fact, the current state of development of AI has long since reached a level where AI can be considered creative and can perform tasks independently and without human assistance.

For this reason, AI is increasingly seen as a driving factor in the Fourth Industrial Revolution, which is characterized by increasing networking and digitization. AI helps to effectively use a company's huge volumes of data, intelligently interlinking the various processes so that, at best, they can run autonomously. AI can learn from a company's data, and recognize trends and patterns in order to use them as a basis for rescheduling production sequences and corresponding processes, further developing the company's own products and services through or with AI, and implementing new types of business models.

In healthcare, AI can be used to aggregate and analyze vast datasets in the form, for example, of medical records and images, population data and clinical trial data, to derive patterns and insights that humans could not find on their own. This supports the entire medical staff in decision-making and optimizes treatment success.

In the transport sector, autonomous driving is currently attracting a great deal of attention. The AI systems used in this context are already capable of dealing with the complex scenarios in road traffic by perceiving their environment and reacting appropriately to it.

Increasingly, research and development is also benefiting from the use of AI. This is primarily due to the potential of AI to learn from data, to discover unknown correlations and patterns, to predict the effects of modifications, and to solve problems independently. Such systems are being used, for example, to develop new vaccines, designing new chemical compounds, simulating their effects and predicting entire complex biological processes, so significantly reducing the number of practical tests.

AI in the patent system

Against this backdrop of AI's growing significance, it is not surprising that the creative potential of AI is also gaining more and more importance in the patent system. Here, there are clear advantages with regard to prior art searches and with regard to the administration of intellectual property rights. Increasingly, however, AI is also gaining importance as a patent subject in computer-implemented inventions or as a means to invent.

Faster, more efficient patent search

AI is already being used as a tool for prior art searches. The AI of modern search tools allows identifying documents that are similar to the description of an invention. In doing so, AI is able to abstract and detach itself from the concrete technical terms of a patent application. In this way, it can identify documents that use completely different terminology but still describe similar concepts. The use of AI can thus significantly improve the quality of the examination for protectability and at the same time reduce the time required for the search.

However, it is not only patent offices that benefit from the use of AI-based searches. Companies often invest large sums in the development of new technologies and products and therefore have a strong economic interest in not interfering with other people's property rights. This is where there is great potential for the use of AI.

Unlike a human, an AI can research and analyze a very large number of patent documents in a short time, even in foreign languages. With the integration of an AI that is able to grasp the meaning of patent claims and compare them with a concrete development, IP rights that might hinder the development, manufacture and launch of a new product can be identified much more efficiently.

AI-based patent management software has the potential to automatically capture patent documents and recognize relevant key information within those documents, making patent document management more efficient: from automatic classification of patent applications to automatic completion of electronic files and calculation of deadlines.

AI patent applications

Already, the rapidly increasing number of AI-related patent applications is presenting patent offices with a capacity problem. In the meantime, due to the interdisciplinary use of AI systems, AI-related inventions can be found in almost all fields of technology. AI-related patent applications can be roughly divided into inventions that have AI as their subject-matter and inventions in the creation of which AI is involved.

AI as an object of invention

AI usually involves computer code, ie, mathematical algorithms implemented in software, where the code is executed on a computer. Patent protection can be obtained for such a computer-implemented invention if, among other things, it has a technical character. This means that an invention in the field of AI may be patentable if it solves a technical problem and achieves a technical effect. For example, patenting of an AI may be considered if an AI is applied to process traffic-camera images and to control an autonomous vehicle by the environment it identifies. In addition, the substantive patenting requirements must be met. The invention must be novel, involve an inventive step and be susceptible of industrial application.

Inventions by means of AI

AI systems today are quite capable of generating new technical solutions that meet the requirements of patentability from an objective point of view. In view of these developments, companies are increasingly asking themselves the following questions:

- Can a patent application be filed for an invention to which an AI has contributed or which an AI has made itself?

- Can an AI be granted the right to be an inventor?

- Who owns the rights to the invention?

AI-related inventions fall into the following three categories:

- Inventions that are made by a human and where AI is applied to verify the result.

- Inventions where a human identifies a task and uses AI to find a solution.

- Inventions where AI identifies a task and provides a solution without human intervention.

Inventions in the first two categories use AI merely as a tool to develop a solution. The third category requires a strong AI that has developed its own comprehensive intelligence. Such AI is not available, at least not yet.

In principle, inventions in all three categories are eligible for patent protection as long as they meet the requirements of novelty, inventive step and industrial applicability. In the case of inventions by means of AI, however, the question arises as to whether the human being or the AI is the inventor and as such can be the bearer of the corresponding rights and obligations.

The European Patent Convention (EPC) requires that the inventor named in the application be a human being and not, for example, a machine. According to the previous view, machines are not legal entities and therefore cannot exercise the rights and obligations of the inventor, in particular, they cannot transfer the rights in the invention to a legal successor.

This view was challenged during the application procedure of European patent application EP 18275163.6. The subject of the patent application is a beverage container with a wall that has a fractal profile (geometric pattern) with a series of fractal elements on the inner and outer surfaces. The elements form indentations and protrusions in the profile of the wall. The profile enables coupling of multiple containers by interlocking the indentations and protrusions on corresponding containers.

The applicant explained that the invention was made by a machine called Dabus. Dabus, he said, was a type of connection-oriented AI from which he had acquired the right to the European patent as an employer. He argued that the machine should be recognized as the inventor and that the applicant, as the owner of the machine, was a legal successor to all IP rights created by that machine.

The European Patent Office rejected the application. The statements that the applicant had acquired the right to the European patent from Dabus as an employer did not meet the requirements of Article 81 and Article 60(1) of the EPC. AI systems or machines can neither be employed nor transfer rights to a legal successor. AI systems or machines do not have legal personality and cannot be party to a contract of employment limited to natural persons. Instead of being employed, they are owned. In addition, AI systems or machines cannot have a legal right to their output that could be transferred by law or agreement.

The applicant appealed, which was dismissed by the Legal Board of Appeal at the oral proceedings on 21 December 2021 (J 8/20). The Legal Board of Appeal confirmed that under the EPC the inventor must be a person having legal capacity and that a statement on how the applicant obtained the right to the European patent must mention the inventor's successor in title. The reasons for the decision have not yet been published.

Thus, if the AI is named as inventor in a patent application, it is to be expected that the patent application will be rejected due to non-compliance with the formal requirements of the EPC's Article 81, Rule 19 (1). Rather, from today's point of view, it seems reasonable to name the human who uses the AI as the inventor of the actual computer-generated invention.

Outlook

Currently, only natural persons can be registered as inventors. The AI is not a legal entity. Inventions generated by means of AI require a user who uses it as a tool, recognizes the results as an invention, establishes its industrial usability and applies for its protection.

The development of AI is progressing steadily. If, in the future, AI should reach the technical level where it is no longer used only for clearly defined applications, but develops its own comprehensive intelligence as strong AI, then fundamental legal and ethical questions will arise, such as the legal capacity of AI and its status in society. Questions of transparency and traceability, as well as the social acceptance of AI, should nevertheless accompany technological developments to a decisive extent.

As patent attorneys at Uexküll and Stolberg, **Philipp Kühn** and **Martin Jacob** assist and advise clients in the field of technology. Their practice focuses on the filing, defence and enforcement of national and international patents and utility models before the relevant authorities and courts.

Uexküll & Stolberg is a mixed partnership of patent attorneys and attorneys-at-law with headquarters in Hamburg and an additional office in Munich. For more than 60 years, Uexküll & Stolberg has represented clients from all over the world in all IP matters before the competent offices and the German civil courts. In addition, Uexküll & Stolberg also provides comprehensive advice in related areas of law, including unfair competition, copyright and contract drafting. Further details at: www.uex.de.

12.
AI, PERSONALIZED
MEDICINE AND IP

Medical innovation is being transformed by a combination of genetic profiling and artificial intelligence, so make sure your intellectual property is up to speed, say Christian Heubeck and Stephan Jellbauer at Weickmann

Genetic profiling is already transforming medicine. Now its effects are being accelerated by artificial intelligence, opening up the prospect of more individual treatment for each of us as patients.

Physicians can currently make a diagnosis based on their knowledge of perhaps a few thousand cases using a limited number of biomarkers as parameters. AI takes this process much further. It can review millions of cases with perfect recall, analysing multiple parameters, which can include visible markers (phenotypes), as well as genetic markers up to a complete profile. Medicine is becoming more personal to each of us.

Conditions are no longer just grouped together as one, such as skin cancer, but are identified in all their different variations. AI gives us the chance to track many more of the complex interactions between genetic mutations. Treatments can then be designed to combat each variation in a way that best suits each patient by ensuring an effective treatment on the one hand and reducing unwanted side effects on the other.

It overcomes one of the enduring challenges in life-threatening conditions, such as cancer, that treatments often only work in less than half the cases and can have uncomfortable side effects. AI opens up the possibility of combining treatments in a way that is less invasive and minimizes the risk of losing time.

Previously, you might combat a tumour, for example, by binding antibodies to it or by flooding the whole body with chemotherapy. Now you might modify an immune cell, such as a T cell, and return it to the patient, using highly tumour specific antibodies or even combining such specific antibodies with a chemotherapeutic and targeting it directly at the tumour.

The hope too is that more can be done to stop conditions happening in the first place. Abnormal patterns in cells, for instance, can be more easily identified by AI imaging rather than relying on a check-up with a physician. Such screenings, when performed as a routine measure by a machine, could significantly reduce costs compared to the case where a physician performs it. Also, it could lead to more targeted treatments before the condition even starts, based only on the vulnerability of each patient.

AI is also advancing the ability of patients to take a more active role in managing their own conditions. In the aftermath of the Covid-19 pandemic, those suffering from psychotic disorders had a long wait for therapy in many European countries. To at least do something before actual therapy by a physician or psychiatrist can start, one option is to use a digital health application. Patients may be prescribed the use of a certified app powered by AI that asks them questions about their symptoms and gives them solutions programmed to respond to their individual experience. Such applications are gaining more and more support from health insurers who see the value in funding them.

Transformational innovation

We are now at the start of a whole series of transformational innovations in medical technologies. However, we cannot expect them to happen based on the classic models for discovery and commercialization. The process of medical innovation itself is changing and the eventual winners may not be who we expect.

There will be scope for disrupters, of course, but the balance of risk and reward is shifting towards those who manage the data on which AI depends. Twenty years ago, for instance, Illumina was just another biotech start-up. Now, it is one of the leading global players in medical data.

However, it is far from inevitable that existing industry structures will be replaced. Outcomes will revolve round two questions: who can master new ways of innovating inspired by AI? and who can adjust best to managing the asset on which medical innovation ultimately depends for realizing its value: intellectual property?

Innovating with AI

Computer modelling is transforming medical innovation. Previously, you first conducted a long process of research and trials, before launching an initial version. Only then would you start to gather insights into how it was performing. In many cases, of course, innovations never reached this point, overcome by any number of points of failure.

Now at the start, you can use AI to survey thousands of existing treatments against your target structures, such as proteins. You can then use a series of specific simulations to see what works best. You then may have a few compounds left that you can test in the lab and modulate the effects on the receptor.

Such modelling lets you synthesize compounds that are already known or might be even new and then delay live tests until much later. One example of such innovation is where immune cells, such as T cells, from a patient are isolated and then re-programmed to treat a specific condition.

As a result, innovation will look and feel significantly different. Less time and resources will be necessary in the lab, as experimentation by trial and error is replaced by more computer modelling and simulation. One effect is that less reliance will be placed on live testing and it will only happen much later in the process.

IP in the AI age

To a high degree, medical innovation relies on the capture of IP to secure its value and its transfer into practice. Otherwise the whole chain of value falls apart. However, if the dynamics of medical innovation have changed, do our assumptions still hold about patents as the preferred route for securing the value in inventions? Or is it better to consider alternatives to keep pace with disruptive competitors whose models rely on data?

We began to see the outlines of what models might emerge in response to the pandemic. Without the use of computer models, it would have been next to impossible to target such a specific part of the virus as its spike. Trial and error in the lab would have taken too long. Moreover, IP proved that it was equal to the task of moving at the speed that today's blockbusters require. It created the foundation for all the partnerships that formed and operated on an express schedule.

As of today, it appears that patents will remain integral to medical innovation for the foreseeable future. However, a series of questions are coming into view about their extent and use. For now, answers tend to vary depending on where you are located. We are in the midst of a deep transformation, after all.

AI as inventor

Given the central role that AI now plays in medical innovation, questions are being raised about the extent to which it can be regarded as an inventor itself. In Europe, a test balloon was launched in 2018, when an application was made for a new type of food or beverage container, designating an AI system called Dabus as the inventor. It was refused by the receiving section of the European Patent Office on the grounds that a machine cannot be an inventor. It has to be a human. The decision was upheld on appeal by the Legal Board of Appeal. So in Europe, for now, a computer cannot be an inventor for lack of legal capacity. A corresponding case had a similar outcome in the United States. However, it is still an evolving landscape. In Australia, a federal court had ruled, for instance, that AI can in effect be an inventor, and this decision has only recently been reversed by a higher instance, the full federal court. So it currently seems that we are starting to see the leading IP jurisdictions come into line with each other.

AI exceptions

In Europe, it's generally assumed that software inventions are excluded from patents unless they show a technical effect. While there is a body of case law when this requirement is met for computer-implemented inventions there is no specific chapter about AI in the EPO's guidelines.

In the case of personalized medicine, AI can involve collection of data, its processing, its modelling and its analysis. So, at each point, AI has the potential to solve a technical challenge and have a technical effect, making it eligible for a patent.

Therapeutic and diagnostic methods

Further exemptions apply to therapeutic and diagnostic methods. These apply with particular force in personalized medicine, because its diagnoses are inevitably based on biomarkers. The case law is evolving here too: the limitations apply to diagnoses on the human body. However, if a device is measuring a variable, such as blood pressure or oxygen saturation, those parameters could well be acceptable.

The challenge is to overcome the limitations on the patenting of methods, both in AI and diagnosis. So, ideally, you will apply for a compound or treatment that can be physically grasped or 'held in hand'. As an outcome, this technical object or effect is protected, but the method is left outside a claim, keeping it a trade secret instead.

Prospects for securing patents in personalized medicine are brighter in Europe, where various ways are feasible for obtaining protection, than in the US. For example, the provision of medical diagnosis for identifying a patient sub-population to be treated can be acceptable in Europe. In the US, it remains more unlikely after negative rulings by the Supreme Court in the Prometheus and Myriad cases.

Freedom to operate

Apart from the challenging legal framework, the scope of patents in personalized medicine, as in other technical fields, depends on how competitive the landscape is. If it's open, then you can look at making a broad claim. If you already have five to six competitors, you are better to target a niche. It can be hard to judge how inventive you are being, however. Personalized medicine is evolving rapidly as a technology and an analysis of patents has a gap of 18 months before you can see what else is being filed. Early filing of an application can be an important step, but the timing must always consider the data available to address potential objections for lack of written description or support.

Territoriality

AI by its nature is boundless. IP, however, is always based within a jurisdiction. So the decision of where you develop certain aspects of your personalized medicine could depend on whether your IP can be protected or not. Equally, you will have to take account of whether you will be able to enforce the rights in your innovation once it is launched.

Other IP

In enforcing IP, patents remain the securest option. However, they are not the only one. If you have programmed an algorithm to identify or monitor a disease for which patentability seems questionable from the start, you might choose to rely on copyright, particularly if speed to market is what counts. Patents take time to set up and in most cases require substantive examination, whereas copyright is almost instantaneous.

Alternatively, if you are the first mover in the market, if you have a good story to tell or if you create a compelling interface with users, then trade marks or designs can give you a powerful source of advantage.

Data rights

One point to remember when innovating in personalized medicine is how far it rests on the genome sequencing of individuals, the use of other biomarkers or other personal data of individuals. You always have to rely on them giving their consent as patients. Data protection is an important issue in this context that must not be underestimated, particularly in Europe.

As the benefits of personalized medicine become clear, hopefully those consents will fall naturally into place. However, even in the age of AI, medicine will always remain a distinctly human experience.

Conclusion

Automated phenotyping, genetic profiling and AI are transforming our experience of medicine. A wave of innovations is coming in how conditions are diagnosed, how treatments are prescribed and how patients manage their own health.

The classic process of medical innovation is evolving as well. The economics of computer modelling are often proving more attractive than experimentation by trial and error.

As yet, we cannot be sure whether the winners will be the leading medical players, disruptive newcomers or data managers. Whoever they are, we do know that they will be those who can find the value in personalized medicine and who use IP to establish it as an asset.

Christian Heubeck and **Stephan Jellbauer** are actively involved in working at all points in the chain of medical value, mapping out the territory that IP in general and patents in particular can occupy when innovations rely on genetic profiling and AI. They are partners at one of Germany's leading IP practices, Weickmann, where they work with a mix of research bodies, innovative ventures and the leading bioscience players. Further details at: www.weickmann.de.

13.
CLIMATE IP

Under the European Green Deal, €1 trillion is being invested in technology supported by strong intellectual property. Sarah Dahl at Grund reviews the potential for early-stage innovation

Extreme weather events, rising sea levels, warming of the ocean, the melting of polar ice, constant threats to forests from drought and ongoing devastating coral mortality are just a few of the effects of seemingly unstoppable climate change. However, not only climate change, but also a notable loss of biodiversity, ozone depletion, water pollution, urban stress, waste production and greenhouse gas emissions represent a few examples of human-caused major environmental issues that we face today. It is inevitable that if the causes leading to such environmental stressors are not massively reduced, our world will experience irreversible harm.

In order to stop human-caused environmental devastation, the European Union has agreed to achieve a lofty goal: to become climate neutral by the year 2050. The assumption is that this future needs to be invented. Under the European Green Deal, €1 trillion is being targeted at technologies with a strong IP position, in particular high-quality patents.

In all fields of sustainability, hurdles must be overcome based on intense research and development projects that will hopefully lead to new, sustainable innovations that will be instrumental in achieving the EU's ambitious goals.

Advantages of patenting green inventions

Studies have demonstrated that strengthening patent protection leads to an earlier commercial take-off by increasing the profitability of firms and providing new incentives for companies to innovate[1]. Moreover, small and medium-sized enterprises in possession of at least one European patent are 34 percent more likely to experience a subsequent growth period and 25 percent are more likely to experience overall growth. Moreover, according to one 2019 study, *High-growth firms and intellectual property rights*, published by the European Patent Office and the EU Intellectual Property Office[2], high-tech SMEs that filed European patents are 10 percent more likely to experience significant growth, meaning over 20 percent revenue growth for at least three consecutive years. Clearly, patents are instrumental for SMEs to market innovations, as well as for identifying external strategic business partners.

Replacing single-use plastics

As part of the European Green Deal, from 3 July 2021, the EU banned certain single-use plastic items (SUPs) from being marketed in EU member states. For example, banned products include plastic cotton bud sticks, cutlery, plates, straws, stirrers, balloon sticks, and polystyrene drink and food vessels. Further banned products include oxo-degradable plastic bags that are marketed as biodegradable but which, according to the relevant EU standards, break down into harmful microplastics that long remain in the environment. These disposable plastics make up around 70 percent of marine litter in Europe.

EU member states have drawn up their own national laws for implementing the SUP directive. Some of them have even decided to supplement the list of banned SUPs. For instance, as part of France's law on the circular economy and the fight against waste adopted in February 2020, most fruit and vegetable packaging will also be banned, as will plastic tea bags, confetti and plastic toys commonly offered as part of children's restaurant menus. In Germany, measures approved in November 2021 added EPS polystyrene food containers to the SUPs included in the directive. In Luxembourg, SUPs have been banned from being sold at festivals from 3 July 2021. Other countries, such as Italy and Belgium, are also on track to introduce a plastics tax or other levy aimed to disincentivize the use of plastics.

Although the various sustainability approaches taken by EU member states may seem haphazard, these policies are in line with the European Green Deal and consistent with the relevant EU regulations that require each member state to develop a waste and pollution-free circular economic model in which any SUPs must be sustainably re-used and recycled by the end of this decade. Consequently, cafes and restaurants will now be forced to stock cups and straws made of bamboo, cellulose or other biodegradable materials for compliance with the various EU regulations.

One example of a successful innovator in green tech is the chief executive and founder of Hope Tree International, who decided to become active in stopping climate change and ocean pollution by replacing SUPs with biodegradable, preferably compostable, alternatives. His initial idea was to provide product solutions that could solve environmental problems without requiring a consumer to change their lifestyle. He started to experiment with different natural and plant-based materials to create biodegradable products based on cellulose. After several years of R&D, the chief executive developed a purely plant-based material useful for producing a variety of single-use products, for instance, cutlery, ice cream spoons, straws, cups, bowls, ear swabs and the like, which can completely replace plastic and paper equivalents.

Although expensive at first sight for a private inventor, the chief executive decided to file a number of patent applications covering all of his innovations. He began by filing several national, German patent applications and European patent applications. After these initial filings, he wisely used the priority year (ie, the first twelve months after the first filing date, during which period subsequent patent applications can be filed while keeping the initial filing date) to identify investors and other sources of funding in order to build a business based on his sustainable yet cost-effective materials with a global IP strategy. At this time, the EU had already announced its SUP ban and its proposed directive was the topic of much lively public discussion and debate which seemed to motivate a number of investors to support Hope Tree International. As Hope Tree was negotiating with possible investors, the pending patent applications were essential in their decision to finance the start-up company.

Part of the capital was deployed in filing international patent applications to secure worldwide protection of Hope Tree's sustainable product innovations, which claimed priority from the early patent filings. For individual inventors, it is challenging to develop an IP strategy, including decisions about which markets to pursue. Certainly, many do's and don'ts must be considered, of which individual inventors are simply unaware. Hope Tree's chief executive reported, for instance, that the nationalization of a patent application in the United States, India or the United Arab Emirates can be a long process extending over many years and can also involve expensive translations. However, despite initially questioning whether pursuing certain markets is worth the money, such markets have proven to be highly profitable for Hope Tree. In addition, the chief executive noted that when a commercial enterprise is just getting off the ground, it can be difficult to foresee in which country the products will be produced and sold. Therefore, it is wise to have the company's IP protected in several countries. He further noted that his IP portfolio is critical in protecting Hope Tree from competitors and companies who manufacture copycat or highly similar products.

This one-time start-up has meanwhile grown to a small-sized company based on the increasing demand for sustainable and environmentally friendly solutions, especially for the global disposable and packaging industry. The company is also increasing its presence with its biodegradable SUPs, especially with businesses located in tourist heavy coastal areas, not least because of the enforcement of the EU's SUP directive.

The chief executive concludes that:

> Nowadays it is undeniable how much interest in environmental protection is growing, especially in Europe. The usual non-transparent and ever-changing dynamics of the politics of different countries has been laid aside given

the environmental crisis. Instead, countries are uniting in a common goal, as highlighted by, for instance, the enforced bans against SUPs. I am proud to actively help in reducing mankind's ecological footprint and ocean pollution. Thus, to me, patents clearly help to implement and realize ideas and inventions in the field of green technologies at a scale large enough to meet the goal of the European Green Deal and the worldwide goal of meeting the 1.5°C target.

The ban on SUPs is one example of the European Green Deal in action. It's on such innovations that the EU is relying to reach its ambitious goals in all the diverse fields of sustainability.

The European Green Deal

The European Green Deal, formally approved in 2020, is a set of policy initiatives initiated by the European Commission with the overarching aim of making the EU climate neutral by 2050. An impact assessment plan is also in the works that aims to increase the reduction in the EU's greenhouse gas emissions that is targeted for 2030, where gas emissions will be reduced to at least 50 percent and towards 55 percent compared with average 1990 levels. The impact assessment plan will also review each existing EU law on its climate merits and further introduce new legislation, including for the circular economy, building renovation, biodiversity, farming and innovation.

Policy areas include:
- Climate action
- Clean energy
- Sustainable industry

- Buildings and renovations
- Sustainable mobility
- Eliminating pollution
- Farm to fork
- Preserving biodiversity
- Research and development
- Preventing unfair competition from carbon leakage

For each, different policies or programmes have been developed. For instance, pollution is the largest environmental cause of multiple mental and physical human diseases, and of premature deaths. Pollution is also a significant driver of biodiversity loss. Accordingly, the EU Commission has proposed a zero-pollution action plan, which intends to achieve a no pollution target from all sources, in addition to providing remedial measures for cleaning the air, water and soil in the EU by 2050.

Sustainable mobility comprises a number of initiatives to reduce transport emissions, which account for 25 percent of the EU's greenhouse gas emissions. The adopted strategy for sustainable and smart mobility lays the foundation for action to transform the EU transport sector, with the aim of a 90 percent reduction in emissions by 2050, delivered by a smart, competitive, safe, accessible and affordable transport system approach.

Under sustainable industry, a policy of sustainable products has been introduced, an initiative which will focus on reducing the waste of materials. This policy aims to ensure that products will be re-used and recycling processes will be reinforced. Materials receiving the greatest attention include textiles, construction, vehicles, batteries, electronics and plastics.

To achieve most if not all these goals, new territories must be explored. Such early-stage actions, are based on a wide spectrum of R&D projects across a variety of technical fields, which ultimately means the development of new inventions.

Financing

The proposed financing of the EU Green Deal is set out in the EU's Green Deal Investment Plan, which comprises two principal financing streams totalling €1 trillion. Over half of this budget, approximately €528 billion, will come directly from the EU's budget and its emissions trading system. The remainder of the funding will be sourced through the InvestEU programme, which combines €279 billion from both the public and private sectors up to 2030 with an additional €114 billion of funding provided by national co-financing. This funding structure will provide an EU budget guarantee to allow the European Investment Bank and others to invest in higher risk projects, thereby enabling private investment. The European Innovation Council has also set aside a €300 million budget for investing in market-creating innovations that contribute to the goals set out in the EU Green Deal.

Based on the European Green Deal, there is and will be enormous EU financial support for inventors acting in one of the above listed fields relating to environmental sustainability. Alternatively, or additionally, there are private investors who are aware of the EU's climate goals and at the same time recognize the commercial importance of inventions grounded in the field of environmental sustainability. Assets relating to green investment funds amounted to $2.7 trillion in the fourth quarter of 2021 alone with significant spending concentrated on technologies designed to offer alternatives to fossil fuels, which were a $755 billion global market in 2021.

All of the EU funding initiatives are foreseen to be invested in technologies supported by a strong IP position, in particular, high-quality patent rights.

EPO support

The EPO is well aware of the current climate situation and has extensively prepared for the surplus of patent applications in the field of sustainability products and processes. Moreover, the EPO helps to raise awareness of innovations in this area.

For instance, on 16 February 2022, almost 7800 participants attended the first ever EPO Tech Day held in public. This online event explored a diverse range of sustainable innovations. The president of the EPO, António Campinos, opened the event by acknowledging that:

> When it comes to sustainability, there are challenges, huge challenges, but we have a patent system that can support the technologies of transformation that will overcome these challenges. We have a patent system that will foster the innovations needed to meet our emissions targets, our recycling and other sustainability goals.

The EPO is thus responding to the increasing urgency of meeting the EU's sustainable development goals by making its services more accessible to SMEs, as well as deepening digital dialogue with all applicants and making patent knowledge available to everyone at no cost via the EPO web portal, Espacenet. Moreover, the EPO offers a new and annual Young Inventors Prize to publicly acknowledge and reward innovators aged 30 or under who are accomplished in the field of environmental sustainability.

In parallel, by the end of this year, the unitary patent and the unified patent court (UPC) will be launched. This is a huge step forward for Europe in terms of the enhanced power to support innovation by providing a single patent right enforceable in all of the signatory EU's member states. This new patent initiative represents the biggest change to patent protection since the signing of the European Patent Convention back in the 1970s.

The impact on green technologies should not be underestimated as many breakthrough technologies are invented by start-ups and SMEs. The lower costs and reduced complexity that the unitary patent offers will be of particular benefit to them. The promise of a single procedure before specialized judges at the UPC will greatly assist in enforcing and monetizing their patents.

These developments will create a true innovation marketplace that promotes licensing and technology transfer between innovating enterprises. These initiatives also provide encouragement for cutting-edge technologies as inventive concepts are realized as commercial products and services in a broad range of transformative technologies.

Dr Sarah Dahl is a qualified European patent attorney, German patent attorney and European trademark and design attorney, who joined Grund IP Group in 2020. She has expertise in all stages of patent prosecution, including drafting and prosecuting patent applications, as well as opposition and appeal proceedings, freedom to operate and patent litigation. In addition to green tech, her technical proficiency extends to inventions originating from the areas of oncology, genetics, immunology, virology, microbiology, molecular biology, biochemical techniques and diagnostics, pharmaceutical sciences, medical computer and software sciences, and related medical devices in the mechanical arts.

Notes

[1] Chu et al. (2020), Effects of patents from stagnation to growth, Journal of Population Economics, vol. 33:395-411

[2] https://www.epo.org/service-support/publications.html?pubid=192#tab3

14.
BRANDS AND DESIGNS
FOR WEB3

The speed at which artificial intelligence, the metaverse and digital wallets are evolving is making brands, designs and copyright integral to realizing the value in digital innovation, says Olivia Petter at HGF

As digital technologies like blockchain, NFTs (non-fungible tokens), 5G, artificial intelligence and virtual reality move towards mass consumption, the question arises whether traditional assumptions about intellectual assets still apply in capturing their full value.

Almost all innovation now relies heavily on these rapidly developing digital technologies. However, it takes time to register patents: from the day of the invention to the grant of a registered IP right, it may take several years. While new technologies have the potential to rapidly change the way we live, shop and feel, it is vital for their creators, as well as their users, to implement a clever mix of IP rights to keep pace with the speed of the developments.

The metaverse

This is especially true for the creation of the metaverse, which deploys several of these new technologies. Like many of them, there is no precise definition of the metaverse. However, it is inspired by science fiction and describes a new form of infrastructure or space on the internet.

Although a lot of these new technologies are based on existing computer science, so that their protection through IP rights poses no new problems, the creation of the metaverse is challenging well-established companies, as well as academics at the moment.

It is argued that the metaverse is the next level of the internet, a virtual three-dimensional world designed on the basis of Web3. Using blockchain technology, Web3 includes concepts such as decentralization and a token-based economy. Platforms to trade and buy NFTs are spreading and new business concepts are mushrooming. Indeed, the creation of a new universe on the basis of a whole set of disruptive technologies is exciting enough to inspire a company like Facebook to change its name.

Generally, innovations require and deserve protection. However, in that context IP rights should not only be seen as a tool of defence, but as a tool to create an asset for the company, a way to describe its real nature. Thus, a holistic approach has to be taken when it comes to the protection of new technology. A mixture of IP rights, which includes not only patents and copyrights, but also trade marks and designs will address every aspect of the innovation.

A good example of that holistic approach is a smart stethoscope, one of the finalists of the DesignEuropa Awards 2021, which is protected not only by copyrights, but also by trade marks and a registered design. The stethoscope is a small handy device, which can be used to examine the respiratory system of a person. It sends the data to a mobile app. Using AI, the software guides the user through the examination and data may also be sent to a doctor for consultation.

The device's outer appearance is protected by a registered design. Its indication of origin, ie, its trade mark, is protected, and the technology involved, namely clever software using AI, enjoys protection through copyright. IP rights are capable of protecting new creations in their technological (patent), visual (design), creative (copyright), and origin-indicating (trade mark) aspects.

Design

Referring to the metaverse as an example again, virtual items and services are intangible by their nature. That is why design rights may become more and more important.

Although trade marks filed lately tend to cover 'virtual goods/ services', it is unclear at the moment whether software relating to downloadable virtual goods is really seen to be similar to real goods in terms of likelihood of confusion under trade mark law.

For example, the Nike shirt in the metaverse is simply a piece of code and thus software, whereas it is a piece of cloth in the analogue world. As digital goods, although marked with the same trade mark, they may not be held to be similar under trade mark law, as their nature, their distribution channels and their use are completely different.

By contrast, designs protect the outward appearance of the whole or a part of a product resulting from the features of the lines, contours, colours, shape, texture, materials and its ornamentation. Not only product packaging may be protected by a design, but also logos, parts of products, web designs, typefaces or get-ups.

In Europe, designs come in two types: unregistered designs which are protected for three years from the date the design was first made available to the public within the territory of the European Union; and registered designs which enjoy protection for an initial period of five years from the date of filing which may be extended to a maximum of 25 years.

When it comes to digital items, it may be that the look and feel of a real product is depicted, whereas the trade mark of the analogue product is not. While the trade mark is protected in relation to specific goods and services, design protection exists independently from the intended use of the design. Thus, a design may be infringed in the same way in the analogue as in the virtual world.

The same is true for copyrights, which not only protect code and software, but also content which may be distributed through virtual reality devices with innovative fields of application. For example, the dentist who is providing a special treatment to patients with virtual reality glasses may become a distributor of copyrighted content. It is further proof of how invaluable an holistic approach to IP rights for innovative products and services can be.

Trade marks

Trade marks are a powerful tool to fight third parties riding on the coat-tails of the reputation and success of a product or service and to indicate the quality and value of one's own products and services. Subject to payment of renewal fees, their protection may be endless.

Once a new app is created and successful on the market, copycats are not far. It is vital in these cases that not only the name and logo of the app are protected by trade marks, at least in key countries of availability, but also that the trade mark rights are enforced as soon as copies are discovered.

As soon as a similar app with a similar name is established on the market and similar trade marks are registered, it is difficult and expensive to get rid of it.

Cancellation actions have to be initiated in different jurisdictions, notice-and-takedown proceedings have to be undertaken on the platforms where the apps are distributed. In the worst case, a co-existence of the similar trademarks has been tolerated for too long with the effect that the trade marks may no longer be cancelled from the registers and may be legally used.

The capabilities of a trade mark to transmit the quality and reputation of a product or service become even more crucial in relation to digital products and services which are intangible for the consumer. Their physical composition cannot be felt as they were before when purchased on the high street. This does not only apply to the online purchase of, for example, a Louis Vuitton bag, but even more so to the utilization of a banking-as-a-service provider or the establishment of your e-wallet. The guarantee of quality which is transmitted by a trade mark really counts when it comes to a service that requires the trust of the consumers and happens in a virtual environment employing new technologies.

The e-wallet issued by an established bank whose trade mark enjoys a trusted reputation will most likely be relied on by more customers than a service offered under a new name without a similar guarantor. A trade mark that guarantees the commercial origin of an e-wallet may also guarantee security and trust at the same time, serving as a valuable asset of the company offering these services.

Although other factors, such as the decline in cash payments due to the pandemic, accelerated the popularity of e-wallets and digital payments, advancements in digital technology and security has made possible the steep rise in use of digital payments in Europe during the last year.

Following the European Commission's proposal for a European Digital Identity in June 2021, digital wallets will become more widespread. They will supersede mobile payment, giving users the option to prove their identity and share electronic documents. Companies will be able to offer a variety of new services with the help of this new secure, transparent and borderless European means of digital identity.

As so many innovations are based on digital technologies, it comes as no surprise that the most popular class of goods in 2021 for trade mark filings was class 9, covering a vast array of computer and software-related goods again, followed by retail and advertising services in class 35.

Copyright

Copyright, from the moment of creation, protects works such as books, articles and other written works, paintings, music and computer programs, to name a few. Copyrights also offer protection to software and non-creative collection of data in case it is subject to significant investments.

Thus, in view of fast-developing digital technologies, copyrights offer a suitable means of protection as they come into existence quickly and may be enforced without delay. However, technologies also take their toll on copyrights, leading to new questions about whether human creation is necessary to copyright a work and whether AI-generated works also enjoy copyright protection.

While the common understanding at the moment seems to be that only original works reflecting the intellectual creation of a human being may be protected under copyright law, it may also be necessary to take into account the consequences of this approach.

A journalistic article, a piece of music or some art which has been created exclusively by AI may not enjoy copyright protection. Accordingly, it is necessary not only to address the output produced by the new technology, but also the input. Without input, AI cannot produce any output.

Thus, case law commonly examines works on a case-by-case basis as to the amount of decisive influence of a human author to it. Of course, new questions concerning the application of IP rights arise, in the case of when new technologies and concepts are combined. For example, software code generated by AI may use open-source software and thus would have to be made available itself as open-source software again.

Territorial scope of IP

The territorial scope of IP rights causes additional problems. Websites, for example, are accessible anywhere in the world. Companies wishing to expand their business on either side of the Atlantic, for example, may also face problems when it comes to the use and protection of their IP rights.

IP rights registered nationally enjoy protection within the borders of that territory. Some IP rights may extend to a larger territory than that of a nation, for example, EU IP rights, as well as international treaties and agreements, such as the Paris, Berne and Hague Conventions, which mutually acknowledge the IP rights of other nations. In taking account of such territoriality within a holistic IP strategy, bear in mind that case law in different regions of the world offers different concepts and conditions on how to deal with the infringement of IP rights on the internet, which may have an effect in the relevant territory.

In a recommendation adopted in 2001, the World Intellectual Property Organization determined that: 'use of a sign on the internet shall constitute use in a member state for the purposes of these provisions, only if the use has a commercial effect in that member state'. Different factors are relevant to the examination of that 'commercial effect' of the use of a sign on the internet.

Considering these factors when examining the use of trade marks and designs in the metaverse or for NFTs, these platforms will most probably also have to install a notice-and-takedown mechanism ensuring that they comply with IP laws in countries where their services are accessible and have commercial effect.

There are also voices which explain that the territory of the website where the metaverse is hosted will most likely be the connection point to the relevant territory. The territorial scope of IP rights thus may not only pose a problem for those entities offering digital services on the internet, but also for those who try to expand their market by distributing their goods through an online shop.

As soon as the goods and services protected under IP rights are offered across national borders, there is a risk that either assets are no longer protected or third party rights are infringed. Companies which were established on either side of the Atlantic first and later on wanted to expand their markets, often with the help of the web, to the other side of the Atlantic frequently face problems, because identical or similar trade marks are registered already.

In case further aspects come into play, such as the language in which the goods or services are offered, the relevant territorial market may be limited to the area in which the respective language is spoken. For example, printed matter, whether it is published on paper or online, may be relevant to a public which speaks a specific language only. Then IP rights protected in specific territories may be sufficient.

Therefore, it is crucial to think of a comprehensive strategy of protection which involves any expansion plans in the future and to consider the accessibility of products or services provided via online distribution.

Conclusion

For entrepreneurs, a good mixture of IP rights not only secures the success of the business and prevents copycats, but also serves as a significant asset in valuing the company. Not only patents may be subject to licensing, but also trade marks or designs can serve as a powerful lever in negotiations with investors and licensees.

Although it is not possible to protect the idea itself, IP rights protect almost every aspect of a new product or service. While a patent protects the technological side of the innovation, trade marks serve as an indicator of the commercial origin and quality, and designs protect the outward appearance of the product or the web design of the online shop where the product or service may be purchased.

Accordingly, the creation of a strategy in terms of IP rights should take into account the following factors:

- IP protection as a valuable asset and cornerstone of any business.

- A good mixture of all IP rights, including trade marks and designs.

- Consideration of ownership of rights and licensing strategies.

- Territorial aspects of the accessibility of the goods or services of the company, as well as potential expansion plans.

Taken together, these IP rights will give protection and value for Web3 innovations, when applied in a holistic manner.

Olivia Petter is an attorney-at-law at HGF in Munich, one of Europe's leading intellectual property firms with 22 offices in seven European countries. She has nearly 15 years of European work experience at different law offices, advising on all matters relating to IP, competition law and commercial law, specializing in creative, media & entertainment, food & drink, healthcare and retail. She publishes regular articles about IP. Further details from: www.hgf.com.

15.
IoT, CONNECTIVITY AND SEPs

Innovate by connecting products to the internet of things, but don't get lost in the maze of standard essential patents, say Sebastian Ochs and Olivia Nemethova at Grünecker

Many in the automotive industry were taken by surprise when the first complaints reached them about an alleged infringement of standard essential patents (SEPs) for connectivity by their cars. Traditionally, SEP disputes were either amongst competitors in consumer electronics, such as mobile phone manufacturers, or patent pools and non-practising entities (NPEs) against consumer electronics manufacturers.

As cars become more a smart phone on wheels, the actual functionality of driving from A to Z is less a selling factor than connectivity and convenient use of external devices. Suddenly, car manufacturers became an attractive group of future licensees for SEP owners. Their thinking was reinforced by the dwindling returns in traditional sectors like consumer electronics and the relatively high selling price of cars as a basis for royalty calculations.

You might think that car manufacturers were used to patent disputes. While it is true that they know how to litigate them, the actual playground has changed. It is now no longer primarily in mechanical engineering, but in a field where they have less experience, electrical engineering. Furthermore, car manufacturers do not really have their own patents that they could assert in return. So it makes it hard for them to react, when they find themselves forced outside their comfort zone.

The major car disputes will at some point come to an end. The next wave of SEP litigation will then loom on the horizon. All manufacturers now have to include electrical engineering into their mechanical products, notably in connecting to the internet of things (IoT). This chapter reviews the circumstances and challenges of these SEP negotiations, highlighting how manufacturers can react in these novel situations.

IoT standards

IoT can be deployed in various scenarios including connected vehicles, eHealth, home automation, energy management, public safety, industrial process control and smart cities. For different scenarios, different standards may be applicable. There is no single standard for IoT. For example, standards supporting connectivity may be communication standards such as ZigBee, WirelessHART, 6LoWPAN, Bluetooth, wi-fi, DECT, cellular communication standards for machine type communication, or wired interface standards. Further standards that may be applicable include compliance, networking, data, and security protocols, such as CoAP (Constrained Application Protocol) or DDS (Data Distribution Service) etc. Another technology field that may be relevant for IoT is wireless charging, largely dominated by the Qi standard.

Particularly in the field of data protocols, there are standards intended to be open in the sense that no royalty needs to be paid to implement them. However, a standardization organization cannot force its non-members not to enforce their patents. Accordingly, even when implementing an open standard, there is a residual risk that it may be covered by a patent.

An asymmetrical IoT game

The particular challenge that implementers may face is that making an IoT product, or merely adding connectivity features, can result in an asymmetrical situation. If a company that has its origin in mechanical engineering is now confronted with a less familiar field of technology, such as electrical engineering, and different opponents, namely NPEs or operations from a totally different sector, it creates a series of challenges that present themselves in ways that they might not originally expect.

New players

SEP owners or licensing entities are typically either market participants from the electronical engineering market, such as consumer product manufacturers, or NPEs and licensing pools. These new players do not only have a different understanding of their own technology, they also are in a totally different position.

Typically, they do not produce anything the mechanical engineer manufactures. Hence, any counterattack on the basis of patents owned by the mechanical engineer cannot be made.

When looking at NPEs and the pools, the situation is even more difficult. Since they do not have any product other than other patents they want to license, counterattacks on the basis of patents are non-existent.

New playground

IoT and connectivity are not closely related to mechanical engineering. Their implementation, at least at the current stage, is by use of third parties, such as integrated circuit manufacturers and suppliers and other vendors that provide the compatibility and interface to the already existing product.

For instance, products that were mainly mechanical now get an add-on, making them suddenly compatible with a wi-fi, Bluetooth or even LTE standard. The issue is that this technology is typically something that is not yet a familiar field for the implementer. In most cases, particularly for smaller companies, such functionality is bought from an external vendor and is not something it has created from scratch itself. So an understanding of the technology can be a challenge in itself.

New rules

Another challenging aspect is that SEP litigation has its own rules. The new players who have arrived, particularly NPEs and pools, may have only one real aim: monetization. They are not that interested in getting someone off the market or stopping them using a specific technology. For them, SEPs, which others cannot avoid using, are for monetizing. It is a different attitude to the standard situation where two competitors in the same sector are fighting each other about a specific technology in their daily business.

Another major challenge is that it is not just one or two patents that are asserted against a specific product, but multiple ones, typically in various jurisdictions. As well as significant resources being required to make a defence against such allegations, the risks increase too. The SEP owner only has to succeed in one of its multiple lawsuits, whereas the defending party needs to win them all.

SEP litigation also has a specific characteristic: FRAND (fair, reasonable and non-discriminatory). It springs from courts who want to balance the need of the implementers to gain access to those patents and use the technology to enter the market, but also of course the interest of SEP owners to rely on their patents. It has resulted in a regime or framework, which obliges the involved parties to negotiate a licence that is fair, reasonable and non-discriminatory.

Do's and don'ts

Don't ignore threats, but don't panic

One of the core don'ts is to ignore threats that come with IoT implementation or connectivity. It is true that they can result in significant interference and disruption of the regular business; the good news is that there is no need to panic. In particular, if reasonable parties are involved, there will always be a possibility to settle the matter.

If there is one unreasonable party, the case law is relatively clear, that in such matters, either the SEP owners gets their right or the implementer cannot be subject to injunctive relief, reliefs for destruction and withdrawal from the market.

However, cases where a FRAND objection is successful are rare. In light of the head start the SEP owners have, they can rely not only on significant resources but also point to various decisions in their favour and to a large group of licensees to support that what they believe is an appropriate royalty rate is actually reasonable. So do take these points into account as early as possible.

Do check the landscape

To assess risks, check the landscape of patents in the field that you are entering as early as possible. The SEPs for a specific standard are not static but rather dynamic. Even if a standard has long been established, new patents can be considered standard essential and certain patents will lapse or declare non-essential in the course of litigation. However, keeping an eye on the landscape is something that makes it easier to assess the potential risks and the exposure in this context. As well as using your searching tools, it is also worth gaining an overview of the litigation and the royalties that could be paid.

Do be aware of potential attacks

Being aware of potential attacks is in close connection with knowing the landscape of the patents. Here, it is of particular relevance to get an understanding of who the active players are and how they acted in the past.

Do factor in licensing fees

Even though it may only be a small amount, the licensing fees that may need to be paid to SEP owners can have a significant impact on your margin. Hence, it is advisable to include into your sale price also a specific allocation for litigation, but also to investigate to what extent such licensing fees need to be paid. It will help later if the product is sold and back royalties have to be applied for those which have not yet been licensed.

Summary

IoT requires connectivity which is typically achieved by some standardized interfaces. Accordingly, there may be multiple SEP owners requiring royalties for their patents. Thus, when planning an IoT product, it is advisable to check the landscape and estimate, as far as possible, additional costs resulting from potential negotiation or even litigation with SEP owners.

In any event, implementers must not turn a blind eye to this issue. Even though the whole patent issue around IoT has certain risks, it comes along with some great benefits and may even be a chance for companies that are new to this technology. So don't get lost in the maze of standard essential patents. There is always at least one way out.

Grünecker is a combined firm of patent attorneys and attorneys-at-law with offices in Munich, Berlin, Cologne and Paris. **Sebastian Ochs** is attorney-at-law and associate partner, who handles patent infringement suits in a variety of technical fields. Sebastian has a focus on interferences between patent and antitrust law. He is currently engaged in various litigation matters in the field of electrical engineering, including SEPs. **Olivia Nemethova** is patent attorney and partner at Grünecker. She is an expert in technical IP rights in the field of electrical engineering, in particular wireless communication, networks, signal processing, coding and artificial intelligence. Olivia has been handling patent prosecution, as well as pre-litigation and litigation including cases concerning SEPs. Further details at: www.grunecker.de.

16.
MANAGING THE NEW
EUROPEAN PATENT SYSTEM

The Unified Patent Court and the unitary patent are going live at last, transforming the filing and the litigation of patents in Europe. Jens Pilger at DHS highlights the potential advantages and pitfalls

The European patent reform package is based on two pillars, namely the Unified Patent Court (UPC) and the unitary patent, and is potentially the most important ongoing development in the European patent system in the last 50 years (ie, since the European Patent Office itself was established). The current patent reform package is the result of a decade-long process of formation and development, which for the time being is not at all complete.

Starting in the early 1960s, long before the formation of the European Union, there were efforts to establish a (unified) European patent system, the most significant result so far being the EPO. Since the EPO is older than the EU, it should be kept in mind that the EPO is based on an international treaty between the member states, the

European Patent Convention, and is thus independent of the EU and EU law. Thus, non-EU member states, such as Switzerland or the United Kingdom, are also member states of the EPC.

The original idea had been to create a real European patent (instead of the bundle of national patents into which a patent granted by the EPO is broken down) that is valid for all states of the EPC or at least for all states of the EU and a corresponding European patent court. Such an architecture would enable litigation and/or nullity proceedings all over Europe in just one trial (instead of having a separate trial in each European country on its own, as it is the case at the time being). Clearly, such a system would enormously increase efficiency of the proceedings, leading to savings in time, effort, and money, while, additionally, contradictions between jurisdictions (as happens nowadays) would be prevented. Yet, as will be analyzed in the following, the practical implementation had to go a long and windy road to end up in a one-of-a-kind judicial architecture.

But even though many compromises and unconventional approaches had to be taken up to now, the rise of the UPC (and the unitary patent) will bring changes and challenges to the patent community, for example:

- decide whether pending and new patent applications should become unitary patents or stay with classical European and/or national patents;

- decide which patents in the portfolio should take part in the UPC and which should not;

- decide if patents that take part in the UPC should be further protected by national patents as fallback positions;

- already consider these new options when formulating patent-related agreements.

UPC foundations

The present organization of the UPC can only be understood, when taking into account the basic problems it had during the last decades. Several approaches have been undertaken to build a bridge between the EU and the EPO, thereby establishing a (unified) European patent system. The most important of these approaches were the Community Patent Convention (CPC) and the European Patent Litigation Agreement (EPLA), even though both ultimately failed.

By contrast, for many years there has existed a successful (unified) EU trade mark and design system. EU trade marks or designs are registered by the EU's Intellectual Property Office (EUIPO), an EU agency that is fully embedded in EU law. EUIPO examines and eventually registers a trade mark or a design for all EU member states at once, while infringement proceedings are handled by the member states' national courts.

While this system works well for trade marks and designs, it seemed to be impossible to form a corresponding system for the European patent world. While the EPO uses three languages (German, English, French), the EUIPO uses two additional languages (Spanish, Italian), thereby overcoming language conflicts. Regarding the patent reform package, the project had been blocked for many years by Italy and Spain who did not accept a three-languages-only system. Furthermore, a part of the patent world (in particular the UK) did not wish to form a system that is fully embedded in EU law. A further issue lies in the fact that the EPO is independent of the EU and thus cannot be transferred into an EU Patent Office.

Present architecture

The new system does not replace but complements the existing European patent system. In its present form, the patent reform package has a juridically unique structure in Europe, as well as worldwide. This present architecture reflects the issues identified above and the unconventional way of solving them.

In order to overcome the resistance of Italy and Spain, the other EU member states formed a so-called 'enhanced co-operation' within the EU to proceed with the project themselves, thereby excluding Italy and Spain (ie, a European patent system without Italy and Spain, thereby solving the language issue).

Two EU regulations had then been issued to regulate the unitary patent. While Italy finally joined the project, Spain, Poland and Croatia did not join the enhanced cooperation. Thus, the unitary patent is actually only a European patent with unitary effect (EPUE) for the EU member states of the enhanced cooperation.

The EU regulations contain, nevertheless, essentially no material patent law. The material patent law is transferred instead to an international treaty called the Unitary Patent Court Agreement (UPCA). It has been agreed upon in the UPCA that the member states of the enhanced co-operation will take part in a common patent court, the UPC. The logic behind this unconventional approach had been to exclude the material patent law from the jurisdiction of the Court of Justice of the EU (CJEU), because the UPCA is an international treaty like the EPC, thus independent of EU law.

In summary, the EU regulations regarding the EPUE and the international treaty that establishes the UPC form the two pillars of the patent reform package. Yet, the following issue arises from this construction: while the EU regulations are EU law, the UPCA is independent of EU law, and the relationship between the EU, the UPC and the EPO will remain a juridical challenge. The bitter irony of this development is that it had been mainly the UK that pushed the patent reform package out of EU law and is at the time being, due to its exit from the EU, not taking part anymore in the project.

While the EPO will continue with the grant procedure in the patent reform package and will also be responsible for the grant of unitary patents, litigation and corresponding nullity proceedings will take place either before the central division, a local division (one state) or a regional division (more than one state) of the UPC. The local and regional divisions are specific national courts specialized in patents, for example the Munich and Düsseldorf courts in Germany.

Nullity proceedings (without corresponding litigation proceedings) will be handled directly by the central division. In the beginning, the central division will be located in Paris and Munich only, since London is no longer part of the UPC system. Decisions of the divisions will be appealable at the Court of Appeal in Luxembourg. A further instance may be the CJEU, however, the role of the CJEU in the UPC system is not entirely clear yet.

At the time of writing, the so-called provisional application phase of the UPC has already started, meaning that final preparations are underway to make the UPC function. As soon as Germany deposits its ratification of the UPCA, the UPC can enter into force, which is expected to happen at the end of 2022.

Options and challenges for patent users

Despite the complex judicial relationship between the EU, EPO and UPC, the new system offers a high number of interesting aspects to the users of the patent system. The most interesting aspect is that the UPC will not be only competent for the European patent with unitary effect (the unitary patent) but for any European patent. In the latter case, the UPC shares the competence with EU member states' national courts on a first-come, first-serve basis. Again, there may be issues with EU law to be resolved in this regard in the future, but the UPC stands for the principle that, with one infringement action, a European patent litigation process is possible over all participating EU member states. Nullity of the patent can also be declared in only one proceeding.

Today, an applicant for a patent in Europe has the choice between a European patent (EP), which will be split after grant into national parts, and the national patents. Due to the prohibition of double patenting, an EP national part can only co-exist with a corresponding national patent, when the scope of protection is different. These two filing options will remain with the rise of the patent reform package, yet, there will be a further option, ie, the unitary patent that covers all EU member states, except Spain, Poland and Croatia. A most interesting aspect is that there will be no prohibition of double patenting regarding a unitary patent and a corresponding national patent. It follows that a unitary patent and the corresponding national patents, even if the scope of protection is similar, can co-exist in Europe. This opens up the chance to establish national patents as fallback positions if a unitary patent is revoked in nullity proceedings.

Regarding patent infringement proceedings, the EU member states' national patent courts have had until now exclusive jurisdiction. It follows that each national part of an EP can only form the basis of an infringement process before a competent EU member state's national court. For the unitary patent, the situation will be completely different, because the UPC will have exclusive jurisdiction for unitary patents. Consequently, a unitary patent could be used tactically to avoid jurisdiction of national courts and bundle all infringement (and/or nullity) proceedings into one single trial.

For the classical EP, there will be a special role in the future: proceedings can take place either before the national courts (one or more national trials) or before the UPC (one trial, but only for those national parts, where the corresponding EU member state takes part in the UPC), depending on where the action is filed in the first place. This circumstance should be strategically taken into account, in particular because there will be the option for the first seven years (this time period may be enlarged) to deny the competence of the UPC (the so-called 'opt-out').

In contrast, the competence of national courts for EPs cannot be denied. It will thus be a crucial workload for patent professionals in the coming months to decide, which patents of their portfolio should take part in potential UPC proceedings (by default) and which should not (opt-out). The opt-out is free of charge, but it has to be declared before an action before the UPC is filed. The opt-out will remain over the entire lifetime of the patent, even though the opt-out may end after seven years. For most portfolios there won't be a simple solution. Different factors have to be taken into account, when deciding about the opt-outs.

Further, it may be advisable to take the different options already before the UPC and national courts into consideration, when drafting agreements (eg, regarding licences). Specifically, it should include a clear jurisdiction agreement regarding which patent system would be used by the parties.

Besides an enormous saving of money and efforts (especially in large cases), the UPC may provide further advantages to the patent community. In comparison to German patent courts, where most patent cases in Europe are handled, the court costs of the UPC are significantly lower. Further, it is assumed that proceedings may be fast, eg, one year for each instance. Since there are only two instances (the court of appeal being the second instance) at the UPC, complete patent infringement and nullity proceedings before all instances may be completed in two years after filing an action. At the time being, the average time of nullity proceedings in Germany is around two years. Since there are up to three instances in Germany, the highest instance taking at least two years, one can clearly see how time efficient the UPC proceedings could become.

Further legal hurdles

There may still be issues with EU law to come. It has not been a surprise that Italy and Spain filed nullity complaints against the EU regulations (regarding the unitary patent) before the CJEU. Yet, the CJEU decided in 2015 that these regulations are compatible with EU law. However, at the time being, it is not clear, if the CJEU considers the UPCA to be in accordance with EU law.

In 2013, the CJEU provided an opinion that the original version of the UPCA does not comply with EU law, because the UPC is not an EU member-state court but instead takes away competences from EU member states' national courts. As a consequence of this opinion, and in order to avoid an endless number of conflicts between the competence of the UPC and national courts, the UPCA has been adapted to overcome the criticism of the CJEU. In particular, the current UPCA defines the UPC as being equal to an EU member state's court, accepts the CJEU as the highest instance and excludes non-EU member states from taking part in the UPCA.

Even though the majority of the patent community appears to be of the opinion that the revised, current UPCA is in accordance with EU law, there are a number of EU law experts who doubt that the CJEU will indeed accept compatibility of the UPC with the EU. So far, the CJEU had no occasion to provide a judgement regarding the UPCA, because it is an international treaty and not EU law. This situation will change, however, once the UPCA is in force and may get into conflict with EU law. Besides the UPCA, the EU civil process law (secondary EU law) has been amended to define the UPC as an EU member state court like the Benelux court.

Nevertheless, it has to be kept in mind that the Benelux court is only an instance of harmonizing the law of national courts and not, like the UPC, a court that takes over the responsibilities of national courts. Further, secondary EU law is located below the primary EU law like the treaty on the functioning of the EU (TFEU), which defines the relation between a EU member state's court and the CJEU in Article 267 TFEU in a manner, that may not be applicable to the UPC.

It came as a surprise in 2017 to the IP community that the whole patent reform package project was paused due to a constitutional complaint before the Federal Constitutional Court in Germany. For an incredible amount of nearly four years, the patent community had to wait for the judgement that the patent reform package is indeed in accordance with German law. However, even though this hurdle has been overcome, the Federal Constitutional Court did not on purpose comment on the part of the constitutional complaint that deals with the question of whether the UPC is in accordance with European law. The last may remain a hurdle that will have to be taken in the future.

As soon as the UPC enters into force, there is bound to be a party that files a complaint with the CJEU, arguing that the UPC takes away the competence of a competent EU member state's national court. At this point at the latest, the CJEU will have to decide about the compatibility of the UPCA and EU law. In this respect, it may be encouraging that the CJEU already considered the EU regulations as EU law compatible, even though this was heavily criticized by EU law experts. This circumstance may show that the CJEU is in principle standing behind the project. However, it cannot be taken for granted that the CJEU will accept EU law compatibility of the UPCA and it should be kept in mind, that no one would have expected that the whole project could have been paused for nearly four years, only due to a constitutional complaint in Germany, one of the countries that most actively supported the project.

Outlook

During the decades of its development, the patent reform package has overcome many hurdles such as two nullity complaints before the CJEU (with respect to the EU regulations only), Brexit and a constitutional complaint in Germany. Chances are high that the UPCA will also survive a nullity complaint before the CJEU. Yet, the new system provides interesting new options in addition to the existing system. So patent owners should plan filing and litigation strategies in Europe tactically and reconsider the positions of their present patent portfolio.

The following practical advice may be considered with respect to the UPC and the unitary patent in the future European patent system:

- the new system does not replace but complements the existing European patent system;
- this circumstance establishes changes and challenges that have to be taken into account;

- ignoring these new options should not be seen as an option;
- one should, nevertheless, keep in mind that there may still be issues with EU law to come (even though the constitutional complaint in Germany has been overcome).

Dr Jens Pilger is a German patent attorney and a professional representative before the European Patent Office. He is a partner at the IP firm DHS in Munich and specializes in patent prosecution, especially in the fields of mechanics, chemistry, electronics, and computer-implemented inventions. For further information, email: pilger@dhs-patent.de

17.
NAVIGATING THROUGH PATENT THICKETS

Overlapping patents can stifle innovation. Andrea Schuessler at Huber & Schuessler compares how access to fundamental patents is being managed in three industries

A patent thicket is a group of overlapping patents in a specific industry. This creates a situation in which the owners prevent one another from innovating. The products in question require the use of hundreds of different patented innovations, often with unclear ownership and/or owned by competitors or small independent companies.

In addition to disrupting or delaying potential innovation, a patent thicket can:

- Increase the frequency of patent litigation

- Increase the complexity of licence agreement negotiations

- Encourage more businesses to patent weaker innovations

- Increase the costs of patent transactions

- Reduce profits to innovative companies

- Limit the incentive for businesses to innovate

The telecoms and computer industries are prime examples of patent thickets, but they are also building up in life sciences and pharma. This chapter takes a closer look at three examples. First, in the telecoms and computer industries where standard essential patents (SEPs) are identified and where fair, reasonable and non-discriminatory (FRAND) terms are a measure to enable licensing under fair conditions.

Second, in the pharma field where patent owners may build a patent thicket around one product and enforce the rights vigorously, putting them in a position to determine the licensing conditions.

Third, in the biotech field where a new technology developed by two competing entities lead to a patent thicket which was complicated by contradicting decisions about validity in various jurisdictions. In addition, an unclear number of other patent owners have applications which may or may not be dependent on the fundamental patents of the two pioneers. To solve the whole complex patent and licensing landscape, the establishment of a managed patent pool is in discussion.

SEPs and FRAND

During the last two decades an interactive world has been created which is facilitated by standards based on patented technologies that enable machines and devices to communicate effectively and efficiently with each other. These technical standards allow people to enjoy connectivity, while SEPs protect the rights of the inventors of each technology that is essential to a standard.

Common technological products, eg, smartphones or tablets, must meet many standards and require the patented technology to do so. Manufacturing these standard-compliant goods without employing key technologies covered by one or more SEPs is impossible.

Technologies that are standardized include those that we use every day, for wi-fi, Bluetooth and LTE for our mobile devices, near-field communication (NFC) in smartcards, and other various technologies found in producing video, audio and autonomous driving.

Standards are typically set by standard-setting organizations (SSOs), such as the European Telecommunications Standards Institute (ETSI) in Europe or the Alliance for Telecommunications Industry Solutions (ATIS) in the United States. ETSI focuses mainly on the development of technical standards that facilitate important global technologies. Currently, about 400,000 patent applications have been declared to GSM, UMTS (3G), LTE (4G), and 5G standards at the ETSI's intellectual property database. This includes over 150,000 active SEPs that are implemented in practically all smartphones and tablets that are sold in Europe.

SEPs are typically self-declared by patent-holding companies as essential for the implementation of standards. This means that the declared SEPs are not subject to any kind of review to determine their supposed essentiality. Since there is no screening for essentiality involved, determining a patent's essentiality and the value is usually left to the companies involved in negotiating a licensing agreement.

The basic principle is that manufacturers of standard-compliant goods that use the technology covered by at least one SEP will need to license the SEP(s) from the holders (or owners). Both parties will then negotiate the conditions and fee for using the technology. The outcome of these negotiations is then formalized by a licence agreement that must reflect the FRAND terms.

FRAND terms are basically a method to ensure that manufacturers are able to license and use standardized technology on fair grounds. SEP disputes are often brought up when a patent owner declines to grant a licence or refuses to grant the license on FRAND terms. Disputes between the licensor and licensee will often be brought to various courts around the world, where the judge or jury will determine the FRAND terms and royalty rates for the parties involved.

In July 2015 the European Court of Justice issued its judgement in *Huawei v ZTE*. This judgement crystallizes an antitrust law framework within which SEPs can be enforced. In particular, the court has standardized an explicit set of negotiating obligations to be followed by all parties involved.

As FRAND is a subjective matter, disagreements over the royalty rates in SEP licensing agreements often arise and prolong negotiations. The essentiality of a SEP or SEPs must first be determined and followed by the exact royalty rate the licensee is willing to pay and the licensor is willing to accept.

In the past five years, several court decisions have been made throughout Europe. Taking Germany as an example, particularly the regional courts in Düsseldorf and Mannheim and the competent appeal courts dealing with the implementation of the ECJ judgment, it has been clarified that the patent owner is obliged to provide a technical explanation of the licensed portfolio. In this regard it has been considered as sufficient to provide claim charts in which the claims are presented and subsumed by way of feature analyses.

There is agreement between the courts that there is not only a single FRAND offer to be calculated with mathematical precision, but rather a certain bandwidth within which (multiple possible) FRAND offers may lie. However, in examining whether an offer is FRAND, the

German courts previously used varying standards but now seem to come to one approach. The courts' position is that FRAND compliance must be shown by the patent owner, whereby it is in principle accepted that different methods may be used for determining the offer.

However, FRAND compliance can be positively determined by different methods. A method frequently used by the German courts is a comparison with other licensing agreements concluded by the patent owner.

If the patent owner can argue that it has already signed a number of similar agreements, then, as a rule, FRAND compliance should not be in question. The situation is similar if the patent owner can derive the FRAND compliance of its offer from a generally accepted pool agreement.

Accordingly, it is insufficient for the patent owner to cite only the royalties and the method by which they were calculated. Rather, the patent owner must also explain the background for the offer and why it believes that its offer satisfies FRAND criteria. Mere placebo explanations that have no actual technical substance are not enough.

With respect to the manufacturer's declaration that it wishes to take a licence as a SEP user, the German courts have set the bar quite low. This request for a licence need not even be explicit; it may also result from conclusive behaviour, such as mere participation in licensing negotiations.

By now, reaching a FRAND license relies on both parties having symmetrical information. However, potential SEP users will find it more difficult to obtain transparent and reliable data. That said, having a third-party SEP database, such as SEP OmniLytics, can help build trust between all stakeholders involved. These databases provide data on SEP numbers, deployment status, legal status and technological specification distribution. Such information may facilitate the FRAND negotiations.

AbbVie's Humira monopoly

Unlike the telecoms and computer industries where the technology is driven by several hundred thousands of patents owned by many different patent owners, in the pharma field one patent owner may build up a patent thicket on its own for just one product. One such example is the US pharma company AbbVie for its product Humira. Humira is a monoclonal antibody and was first approved in December 2002 to treat rheumatoid arthritis. Up until now, its use spans 16 indications for adult and paediatric patients.

AbbVie filed about 250 patent applications for Humira in the US, 90 percent of them following the drug's 2002 approval. About 150 of them have been granted. Humira's relatively early entry as a biological product and applicability in numerous indications has allowed for the accumulation of an extensive patent portfolio.

The strengthened patent shield and AbbVie's aggressive stance in pursuing the broad patent portfolio has stretched AbbVie's legal monopoly in the US for six years beyond the expiration of Humira's main patent in 2016. The first biosimilar (copycat versions of biologic medicines) will probably come to the US market in 2023 as AbbVie has entered into settlements with nine manufacturers to allow for a 2023 launch of biosimilars. Nonetheless, some of Humira's manufacturing patents extend to 2034, necessitating other biosimilar manufacturers to pursue individual negotiations and cross-licence agreements with AbbVie in order to launch their own candidates.

Since all patents around this product and its uses are in one hand, Abbvie can more or less dictate the licence conditions and keep biosimilar competitors away. This was attacked by an antitrust complaint brought against AbbVie but was dismissed in June 2020 in a Chicago district court and is currently under appeal in the US Court of Appeals for the Seventh Circuit. The district court decision in favour of AbbVie suggests a patent thicket with the potential to impact biosimilar competition is not in violation of antitrust laws. The story is different in Europe, where biosimilars arrived in 2018 and quickly decreased Humira's market share.

Thus, in the situation with one player having a broad patent portfolio covering the product, licensing appears to be the only possibility. In the best case cross-licensing is possible.

CRISPR's complex patents and licences

On 28 February 2022, the Massachusetts Institute of Technology and Harvard's Broad Institute gained a victory over the CVC group (the University of California-Berkeley, the University of Vienna and Emmanuelle Charpentier) in an interference dispute over genome-editing CRISPR technology. The Patent Trial and Appeal Board (PTAB) of the US Patent and Trademark Office (USPTO) ruled that the Broad Institute was the first to invent single-guide CRISPR-Cas9 gene-editing technology for use in eukaryotes. Furthermore, the judges ruled that CVC failed to provide either sufficient, persuasive evidence of an earlier reduction to practise or conception before Broad's evidence of reduction to practise.

The PTAB's decision is theoretically appealable by CVC. However, pending the outcome of any appeal, this current decision results in Broad having ownership over applications of CRISPR-Cas9 technology in eukaryotic cells. This provides Broad with substantial control over the CRISPR-Cas9 patent landscape because it provides ownership to

Broad of using the CRISPR-Cas9 system to edit the genomes of higher organisms. In Europe, however, the situation is quite different. Here Broad lost important patents due to several third-party oppositions and CVC appears to be in a better patent position.

As mentioned above, the CRISPR technology has an expansive patent estate (about 11,000 patent families according to the agency Centredoc), whereas Broad and CVC hold the most fundamental and strategically important patents. However, various academic institutions and biotech companies hold many related patents in their attempts to turn it into medical success. For these players the PTAB decision has substantial financial ramifications, as these companies have invested millions of dollars in translating CRISPR into medical therapies to treat patients. These biotech companies have either taken licences from Broad or CVC, or will have to do so upon having a market-ready product.

In light of this recent decision of the USPTO, licensees of CVC will now have to renegotiate with Broad for at least the US patents. Moreover, this decision means that a number of CVC's US patents that are directed to using the CRISPR-Cas9 system in eukaryotic cells could be rendered invalid. In the event these patents are invalid, CVC could potentially lose significant licensing revenue for the US market.

In addition, the PTAB's decision may impact other pending interference proceedings. Currently, the companies ToolGen and Sigma-Aldrich are involved in pending interference proceedings in which the USPTO has judged that these companies have pending claims that interfere with the same Broad patents that were in suit in the Broad/CVC interference. Thus, the outcome of these proceedings may further have an influence on the ownership of the CRISPR-Cas9 technology in the US.

The PTAB's decision has significantly impacted the CRISPR-Cas9 patent landscape by awarding significant control of the CRISPR-Cas9 technology of the US market to Broad. The outcome of a potential appeal by CVC, and the outcome of the pending interference proceedings with ToolGen and Sigma-Aldrich, will have an impact on whether Broad retains this control. As mentioned above, the situation in Europe and also other markets is significantly different which complicates the whole licensing situation.

Despite the ongoing patent disputes between both parties, Broad and CVC promote widespread adoption of CRISPR-Cas9 technology. In addition, both organizations' non-exclusive licenses for CRISPR's IP are a sign that they want to maximize opportunities for therapeutic development for human diseases.

To solve the whole CRISPR-Cas9 complex patent and licensing landscape, there have been calls from some industry experts to create a patent pool. Such a patent pool will obviate the need to negotiate different licences from different patent holders, creating a user-friendly marketplace while monetizing the technology for its owners. This could create a win-win solution for both sides. Broad itself has mentioned such a solution in a statement. Broad is open to a joint licensing strategy or patent pools with the hope of ensuring open, equitable and streamlined access to these transformative tools.

This patent pool may be similar to those organized by MPEG LA which managed the MPEG-2 patent pool in the consumer electronics industry. In addition, MPEG LA launched Librassay in 2012, which makes diagnostic patent rights from some of the world's leading research institutions available to everyone through a single licence. Organizations which have included patents in Librassay include Johns Hopkins University, Ludwig Institute for Cancer Research,

Memorial Sloan Kettering Cancer Center, the National Institute of Health, Partners HealthCare, Leland Stanford Junior University, the University of Pennsylvania, the University of California, San Francisco and the Wisconsin Alumni Research Foundation.

Thus, in the situation with unclear ownership of the fundamental patents in different jurisdictions and many dependent patents from hundreds or even thousands other owners, a managed patent pool appears to be a way to solve the problem and to ensure that therapeutic products based on this technology can come to the market.

Dr Andrea Schuessler is a founding partner at Huber & Schuessler, an internationally oriented firm of patent attorneys in Munich, specializing in the life sciences, ie, biotechnology, pharmacy and related technologies. Huber & Schuessler supports its clients in all questions of IP and has extensive experience in the identification of valuable inventions, worldwide prosecution and enforcement of patents, and questions of technology transfer. For further details, e: schuessler@patservice.de, t: 49 (0)89 437 7880 or see www. patservice.de.

18.
SURVIVING THE TROLLS

After 20 years of repelling attacks by classic non-practising entities, Friedrich Emmerling and Karl-Ulrich Braun-Dullaeus at BPDE review what defendants can learn from the cases that have been fought

Non-practising entities or NPEs is used as a generic term for individuals as well as small and large patent aggregators. More colloquially, they are called patent trolls. What NPEs have in common is that they do not manufacture products, but generally hold patents with the purpose of licensing those patents to practising entities, ie, companies producing and selling goods which might infringe the acquired patents in the respective jurisdiction. The licensing process quite often comprises enforcing these patents against the practising entities. The business model of the NPEs has the advantage that the attacked practising entity cannot defend itself by using its own patents, as the NPEs do not have products at all and, thus, cannot accordingly infringe. This unbalanced situation is one of the reasons why these entities are not really beloved by the practising entities. The risks of an injunction or high damages quite often force the practising entities to settle the litigation without ever really having challenged the infringement or the validity of the patents involved in the litigation.

Triggered by the first significant NPE action, NTP Inc against Research in Motion (RIM) in the United States at the beginning of the 21st century (the BlackBerry case), in which a settlement of more than $600 million was reached, the wave of patent litigation finally spilled over into Germany in 2004 with an NPE, Inpro Licensing, suing T-Mobile for the distribution of BlackBerry devices. It was notoriously unsuccessful.

Fuelled by the technological changes in electronic business and, in particular, in mobile communications, patent portfolios were sold giving NPEs the chance to get hold of larger shares of patents. One of these entities was the Munich-based company IPCom buying the patent portfolio of Bosch for the GSM and UMTS mobile standards. IPCom's first target was Nokia, initially dreaming of €12 billion in licence fees, according to Juve Patent. We don't know if there was finally an outflow of cash at all from Nokia in IPCom's direction, however, if there were, it was far, far away from the initial amount.

Even if these amounts have been never reached, the chance of gathering several tens of millions of euros is tempting, in particular if the investments for buying patents and the costs for the attorneys seem to be limited in view of the chance to get royalties from a large number of licensees. The business model of NPEs has therefore followed the money and extended to almost any technical field, such as energy technology, food technology and medical technology. In 2014, it was estimated that the overall damage caused by NPEs is in the region of $60 billion each year (Harvard Business Review, November 2014). It was concluded that they tend to sue cash-rich companies, and innovative new technologies, of course, generate cash.

As a result, a large share of patent litigation is caused by NPEs worldwide, notably in the US. According to Professor Dennis Crouch (Amicus Brief, October 2016), over 90 percent of patent suits brought in the Eastern District of Texas were filed by NPEs established for the purpose of litigating patent suits. At this plaintiff-friendly venue, patent holders win nearly 80 percent of the time as outlined by Larry Downes (Harvard Business Review, June 2017). Of course, such a situation is threatening and too often causes a settlement of the litigation without ever having challenged the patent. Nevertheless, this is specific to the Eastern District of Texas and not applicable to Europe.

Contrary to US jury-based trials, patent litigation proceedings in Germany are decided by a panel of experienced judges thoroughly analysing the infringement and validity of the patents. Therefore, the situation in Europe and, in particular, in Germany is completely different to the situation in the Eastern District of Texas. Even NPEs with larger patent portfolios can be completely or largely unsuccessful. On average one can say that NPEs are far less successful in Europe than in US.

Nevertheless, the chance to possibly achieve an injunction against a defendant makes Germany an attractive venue. Only one patent in the portfolio has to be successful to force the defendant into a licence agreement in view of an injunction.

However, even this possible risk of an injunction should not create the impression that a defence in such a litigation is hopeless. To the contrary, the NPE's way to an injunction is not that easy and a number of conditions need to be fulfilled before the German courts grant one. Not only are these preconditions essential for the outcome of the proceedings, but also many other factors affect the risks in these procedures.

Besides these legal preconditions, we recognize a number of patterns from our technical perspective which might be not true for all NPEs which, however, have been recurring.

Portfolio quality

Frequently, the patents in the portfolio of an NPE have been of questionable quality: either the patents were already drafted at a lower level that you would expect for the respective technology; or the prosecution history was less than perfect, resulting in formal deficiencies of the patents. One presiding judge at a leading patent court venue once expressed his opinion that only low-quality patents end up on his desk, as, for good patents, there is no real dispute whether they are infringed or not.

We often found that the portfolio bought by an NPE largely comprised mass-production patents. Obviously, the company selling these patents wanted to get rid of a bunch of patents which essentially only cost annual fees and will not contribute to the monetization of the patent portfolio. The value of such lucky bags only becomes apparent on a closer inspection.

According to our experience, the companies creating the patents are usually well aware at an early stage whether or not a respective invention might become relevant later. Therefore, highly relevant patent applications are handled with more financial efforts, ie, more care than the probably not so relevant patents. Thus, the sold mass-production patents often bear a higher risk of potential deficiencies compared to the patents which the company keeps for its own monetization efforts.

Moreover, patents of NPEs often pass through many hands via opaque and, in retrospect, difficult-to-trace routes until they arrive at

159

the NPE starting the litigation. In such a case, it often proves extremely difficult for the NPEs to prove their entitlement.

Thus, according to our experience, we could already observe a relatively large number of cases experiencing problems with entitlement, assignment, priority right, added matter etc. In this context, we would like to address a difference between a classic NPE and one with a patent pool. The NPE with a patent pool usually acts as the administrator or as a one-stop shop for licensing a specific technology. These pools may be joined by the key players in this technology. In such a case, a much higher quality of the patents should be expected.

Evaluating claims

This leads us to another important point when defending against NPEs. In most cases, NPEs have not drafted and prosecuted the patents by themselves but just bought them from other companies.

If these IP rights were then only sold with rudimentary claim charts, the NPEs have to take care of a proper evaluation of the potential infringement themselves. This is time-consuming and expensive, particularly if the NPEs do not have the proper resources with deep technical knowledge in the respective technology.

In such a case, a number of NPEs did not put much effort into the necessary evaluation of the infringement situation, but started the proceedings on the basis of several patents in an approach based on trial and error. It could make sense economically, if the costs for acquiring and evaluating the patents were low and the expected licence fees are far more than the potential litigation costs.

Therefore, patents used in such a trial-and-error strategy may suffer from the fact that they do not clearly cover the attacked embodiment.

Thus, a thorough infringement analysis of the situation may well reveal that the NPE's attack was not justified.

We observed this particularly in the field of standard essential patents (SEPs). When technical standards are developed, many contributions to these standards are made for which in most cases patent applications have also been filed. However, as only a few of these contributions are implemented in the standard, there exists a huge number of patent applications and patents which do not really cover the final version of the standard. These huge patent portfolios consume significant amounts of annuity fees, so that it could be that companies try to outsource portfolios of less relevant patents and patent applications to NPEs.

Even if an NPE's patents seem to cover a standard, we often saw the claims trimmed to the standard during the patent prosecution. It usually results in an inadmissible extension of the claims, ie, in invalidity of the patent, or in a more narrowly interpreted claim. As the NPE has to prove both the infringement and the validity of the patent, and the defendant has to disprove only one of these aspects, it often ends in a case being dismissed.

Technical input

In Germany, the initial complaint of infringement doesn't have to prove the infringement seamlessly in a detailed way. So the litigation proceedings may be started with little effort, which makes it attractive for the NPEs to start usually with numerous patents.

However, the workload for the NPE increases drastically, if the attacked company defends itself with the complete competence of its department for research and development. To compete with this technical input is challenging for the NPEs, as they usually do not have their own R&D departments and do not know all of the implementation details.

Thus, once the proceedings have started, the NPE has to afford the necessary human, technical and financial resources in order to uphold its infringement allegations and to defend the patents. As these proceedings may last several years, the NPE needs a respective cashflow during this time. Furthermore, if the NPE loses, it has to bear the court fees and the statutory attorney fees, which might add up to significant amounts depending on the number of patents and the involved value in dispute.

In this context. it might be worth knowing that the maximum court fees for a first instance nullity action add up to almost €500,000. We have experienced before that an NPE claimed the maximum possible value in dispute for its case but disappeared from the European market once the obviously invalid patent was revoked without paying the necessary court and statutory attorney fees.

As the NPEs are financially driven, they are often open to agreements to run away, when it becomes obvious that the patent litigation will not be successful. As their legal advisors sometimes assess the situation differently to the defendant, we would recommend in such a case that the involved company should negotiate directly with the NPE.

Additionally, we can see that NPEs with a less strong financial background tend to sue only one small and assumed weak company in order to keep the financial risk low. Once they are successful with one patent, they use this case for financing other cases with further patents. Thus, it might well be that these NPEs give up once they have lost the first instance in the infringement and nullity proceedings.

Combined defence

In contrast, NPEs with a stronger financial background tend to sue several companies in parallel. Aside from the fair, reasonable and non-discriminatory (FRAND) terms that apply to SEPs, we have the feeling in these instances that NPEs place their trust in defendants having difficulties in aligning their arguments with each other, so that they can use the inconsistencies to their advantage. Even if the different arguments brought forward by the defendants are technically correct, they might offer the chance for the NPE to argue that the defendants are contradicting each other. The NPE's approach could in this way compensate for a lack of technical expertise. Thus, the better the defendants work together, the smaller the area of attack is that they would offer to the NPEs.

Finally, it is the team work in the joint defence group between the lawyers and patent attorneys that leads to a dismissal of the infringement complaint, a revocation of the patent or at least to an interpretation or amendment of the patent, which is no longer being infringed. Relying only on the non-infringement or the invalidity of the patent, would disregard the chances that a squeeze between infringement and invalidity could lead to a more realistic claim interpretation.

We can now see that the patent portfolios of the classic NPEs rarely comprise crown jewels. By no means will an NPE automatically win, if it sues a company for breach of several patents. In this context, it is reassuring to know, that IPCom's crown jewels from the #100 family proved to be bits of broken glass. After twelve years of inconclusive patent battles, the last members passed away peacefully at the beginning of 2020 through infirmity.

Friedrich Emmerling and **Karl-Ulrich Braun-Dullaeus** at BPDE have been at the forefront of NPE actions over the last 20 years, particularly in the electronics sector, where they have acted for a network provider, mobile phone manufacturers and a producer of network components.

19.
IP RISKS FOR INVESTORS

IP is a prime asset for investors in tech ventures, but few realize how vulnerable it is to attack as growth starts to happen. So explore these five questions first with potential targets, says Mathias Karlhuber at Cohausz & Florack

Many investors in technology companies are well aware that their returns largely depend on a potential target's portfolio of intellectual property, so realize it is worth making a close analysis of it. However, they sometimes fail to appreciate that it may not necessarily protect the company against IP-related attacks by competitors in the market, let alone by so called non-practising entities (NPEs) or trolls, ie, companies or research institutions that hold patents and other IP rights, but do not offer any products or services.

It comes as a surprise to them because of the special protective function of IP rights, such as patents. They merely grant a negative prohibitive right, ie, the owner may prohibit others from using the protected creation, such as a patented invention. However, a patent does not provide its owner with a positive right of use for a product.

If this product infringes someone else's patents, its marketing can be prohibited, irrespective of whether the seller owns a patent covering that product or not, so jeopardizing an entire investment. Such a scenario is worth keeping in mind when assessing a target's risks, especially as when growth happens, hopefully boosted by the investment, visibility in the market rises and, hence, the risk of IP-related attacks.

So even if the target company has built up a more or less sizeable patent portfolio, it does not mean that it is protected against patent-based attacks to its products and services. If a target's patent portfolio is only mapped to its own products and services, it typically falls too short in properly assessing the IP-related risk to the investment. Instead, it usually takes:

- an analysis of the IP situation of immediate competitors, as well as other IP stakeholders in the respective field of technology;

- an evaluation of the potential defensive value of the target's IP portfolio;

- and an assessment of the overall litigiousness in the competitive environment.

Such questions asked upfront greatly simplify and clarify the prospects for realizing the value in an investment.

Explore what IP is out there

Irrespective of what kind of attack scenario a target company might be facing, an obvious prerequisite to a sensible IP risk assessment strategy is to obtain comprehensive knowledge about the IP rights which exist and could potentially represent a risk for the target's commercial activities. In the field of patents this knowledge is typically obtained by running a suitable patent database search which provides information about existing patent applications and granted patents. The hits provided according to the search profile chosen then have to be assessed for their relevance to the target's current or future products and services.

The major challenge clearly is to define the right search profile which produces a digestible number of hits which can still be processed within the typically limited amount of time and within a budget that is reasonable in view of the potential investment, yet provides a sound overview of potentially critical patents. Patent database searches generally provide a multitude of arbitrarily combinable options to restrict the scope of the search. Typically, the search profile is technology based using classification schemes, such as the International Patent Classification (IPC). One could, for example, further reduce the number of hits by combining this technology-based search with the names of relevant competitors in the target company's markets or by exclusively focusing on known competitors. The latter however possibly creates risky blind spots for NPEs or yet unknown competitors which might hold or obtain patents in the target's field of technology.

A target with a seasoned IP strategy will already have set up such a search process and profile, typically as a continuous monitoring and risk assessment process where new hits are identified and assessed for their relevance to the target's business. Hence, if possible, the target should be asked for their monitoring profile and existing risk assessment, as a starting point for the investor's own analysis.

It should in any case be noted that such a database search is, of course, only a snapshot of the situation at the time of the search and has a blind spot of about 18 months due to the delayed publication of patent applications after filing. Hence, depending on how long the risk assessment process takes, running the search again towards the end of the process is recommended to catch more recently published patents and patent applications.

It should be further kept in mind that any existing risk assessment made in the context of a third-party patent is only a snapshot based on the target's current commercial activities. As these may change fairly quickly, not least due to the investment, the risk assessment may rapidly become outdated. Hence, such risk assessments should be continuously updated along with the target company's development.

Explore the defensive value of the target's IP portfolio

A further element in assessing the IP-related risk is evaluating the target's resilience against attacks by competitors. This can be done by evaluating whether or not the target's IP portfolio covers aspects of the technology which are attractive to competitors in the market. If such a position has been achieved by the target, any competitor who risks infringing a target's patents will think twice before attacking it. A prerequisite to this preventive effect is that a competitor holding critical patents is itself interested in using the technology covered by the target's patents and therefore willing to enter negotiations. Hence, under this defensive aspect, the relevance of the target's patents to their own products is less important. Rather, the primary value of the target's IP portfolio lies in its relevance to the products of the competition.

A target with a seasoned IP strategy will already have set up a filing and prosecution strategy which does not only focus on its own products but keeps the defensive value of patents in mind. Optimally, the target already has a corresponding charting process in place which analyzes competitor products against the target's patents. Hence, if possible, the target should be asked for their filing and prosecution strategy, as well as their competitor-analysis process.

Explore the target's active IP risk mitigation strategy

Certain targets may even have implemented a more active approach to mitigate IP risks associated with competitor patents in that they try to prevent potentially critical competitor patents from being granted or to attack such patents on grant.

In essence, most of the existing national or regional patent systems provide two ways of attacking patent applications and patents. Depending on the respective national or regional provisions, an attempt to prevent a patent from being granted can be made by submitting third-party observations or, where applicable, by filing a pre-grant opposition with the examining patent office. Challenging a granted patent can either be achieved by a post-grant opposition filed with the competent patent office or by other invalidation attacks, eg, nullity actions, before the competent patent office or national court.

In certain fields of technology or markets, it is a more or less customary preventive practice to file such attacks against competitor patents using typically fairly inexpensive opposition procedures even without an immediate commercial threat.

Furthermore, it should be noted that NPEs are not susceptible to infringement counter-claims. The only possibility to mitigate the risk are attacks to their patents. However, for a certain type of NPE, rather than developing its own patents, it successively acquires interesting patent applications or patents from practising entities to enforce. This is often the case where competitors of the target pull out of certain fields of technology and monetize their related IP by selling it or spinning it off into a licensing entity. Hence, what may once have been the patent of a competitor perceived as less aggressive in the market may well end up in the hands of a considerably more aggressive NPE, the business model of which is to license and, if need be, enforce their patents.

Hence, investors should ask the target for its strategy towards these types of NPE. It will indicate the level of sophistication of its IP strategy and its IP awareness in the market. The target should also be asked if they are aware of any noticeable patent sales by competitors as the latter may be a signal for upcoming licensing activities by the buyer.

Explore the target's licensing strategy

Certain targets may also have mitigated IP risks by entering licence agreements with IP holders. While a target will have to reveal existing license agreements to the investor, it is worth exploring whether the target entered that licence agreement at will or whether it was forced to do so in order to avoid or terminate patent litigation. The latter gives an immediate idea about the litigiousness of the market and the risk of further infringement claims, especially if the market share or commercial success of the target increases.

A special licensing scenario may arise with patent pools, where patent holders pool their patents for a certain technology in order to license them to third parties. Such a scenario is often encountered in the context of standard essential patents (SEPs) which are inevitably infringed if a certain industry standard is to be met. Such SEPs cannot be freely enforced by their owners but are subject to a licensing offer under fair, reasonable and non-discriminatory (FRAND) conditions. Enforcement is only available if the potential licensee refuses to take a licence under these FRAND terms.

While the options for attacking these patents are available in this scenario, the sheer number of patents involved typically does not lend itself to such an approach. As it is typically advisable to assess one's exposure to this scenario and to seek early clarity by obtaining the necessary licences, a target having agreed licences for such patent pools shows a reasonable level of sophistication in their IP strategy.

Explore the litigiousness of the market

A final aspect to be explored when assessing IP-related risks is the overall litigiousness of the market. Certain markets or fields of technology are far more prone to IP litigation than others. Even if the target operates in such an environment, it does not necessarily have to have been involved in such litigation. This may, for example, be due to the current low visibility or market share of the target which makes it an unattractive object for IP litigation. However, that situation may of course quickly change, not least due to the investment.

Hence, investors should ask the target if they have been involved in IP litigation in the past or if they are aware of such disputes in the market as this gives a good indication about the litigiousness of the market and the related IP risks. It should be noted that commercial providers are available to provide statistics and further insight in litigation activities in certain fields of technology.

In any case, investors should not forget that what puts a target on the radar of competitors or NPEs most likely is their commercial success. The main difference between a competitor and an NPE is that the former is more likely to take early action in order to protect its market share, while the latter has good reason to wait until the target has established itself and reached a sizeable market share which makes it an attractive object of licensing activities.

In summary, assessing the IP-related risks of the investment in a technology company is a comprehensive task for the investor which should be based on a thorough understanding to the patent situation in the market. The target should be asked a series of questions which provide the investor with a good initial idea of these IP-related risks, as well as if and how these have been approached by the target in the past. Asking these questions may greatly simplify the IP risk assessment process which is crucial, as successful IP litigation against the target may jeopardize the entire investment.

Mathias Karlhuber is a partner at Cohausz & Florack, a multi-disciplinary law firm in Düsseldorf and Munich that supports its clients in all matters relating to IP and unfair competition. He is an expert in technical IP rights in the fields of electronic program guides, medical devices, semiconductor lithography systems, railway technology, vehicle dynamics, crash safety and aerodynamics, specializing as well in data security, micromechanics and general mechanical engineering. He also served for many years as the rapporteur on patents at the IP commission of the International Chamber of Commerce. Further details at: www. cohausz-florack.de.

ABBREVIATIONS

AI	Artificial intelligence
ATIS	Alliance for Telecommunications Industry Solutions
CJEU	Court of Justice of the European Union
CPC	Community Patent Convention
DIN	German Institute for Standardization
EP	European patent
EPC	European Patent Convention
EPLA	European Patent Litigation Agreement
EPUE	European patent with unitary effect
ETSI	European Telecommunications Standard Institute
EUIPO	European Union Intellectual Property Office
FRAND	Fair, reasonable and non-discriminatory
FTO	Freedom to operate
HTB	High-growth technology business
IA	Intellectual asset
ICT	Information and communications technologies
IMS	Integrated management system
IP	Intellectual property

IPC	International patent classification
IPO	Initial public offering
IoT	Internet of things
IIoT	Industrial internet of things
ISO	International Organization for Standardization
NDA	Non-disclosure agreement
NFC	Near-field communication
NFT	Non-fungible token
NPE	Non-producing entity
PDCA	Plan, do, check, act
R&D	Research and development
SEP	Standard essential patent
SME	Small and medium-sized enterprise
SSO	Standard-setting organization
SUP	Single use plastic
TREU	Treaty on the functioning of the European Union
TRL	Technology readiness level
UKIPO	United Kingdom Intellectual Property Office
UP	Unitary patent
UPC	Unified Patent Court
UPCA	Unitary Patent Court Agreement
USPTO	United States Patent and Trademark Office
WIPO	World Intellectual Property Organization